*The Privilege of
Being a Woman*

The Privilege of Being a Woman

WITH A NEW PREFACE

ALICE VON HILDEBRAND

Sapientia **Press**
of Ave Maria University

Sapientia Press
of Ave Maria University
5050 Ave Maria Blvd.
Ave Maria, FL 34142

Editorial and Production
Dominic Aquila, Ph.D.
Henry Russell, Ph.D.
Diane Eriksen

Cover Image
Fra Angelico (1387–1455), *The Coronation of the Virgin*
Photo: H. Lewandowski
© Réunion des Musées Nationaux/Art Resource, NY
Louvre, Paris, France

Cover Design
Eloise Anagnost

Printed in the United States of America.

Library of Congress Control Number: 2002103817

ISBN-13: 978-0-9706106-7-6

DEDICATED WITH LOVING GRATITUDE
TO MY DEAR FRIENDS WHO
ALL LOVE TO BE WOMEN

Alice Ann Grayson, Barbara Henkels, Joanie Smith,
Wendy Teichert, and Rose Grimm Teichert

Contents

PREFACE ix

PART I
Arguments Against the Privilege
of Being a Woman..1
    Secular Arguments...1
    Christianity and Arguments
    Against Privilege 11

PART II
Arguments for the Privilege
of Being a Woman 15
    The Supernatural View 15

PART III
From Paganism to Modern Values:
Denigration of Woman 23

PART IV
Woman: The Privileged Sex 35
    Cons and Pros of Weakness 36
        Cons 36
        Pros 42

PART V
The Transfiguration of Weakness:
The Incarnation 53

PART VI
Women's Supernatural Mission 59

PART VII
Women and Feelings 67

PART VIII
The Mystery of the Female Body 81
   The Mystery of Femininity 88
   Maternity 95

PART IX
Mary and the Female Sex 99

He who reads Genesis on his knees, should be impressed by the privileged position granted to Eve from the moment of her creation. Not only her body — taken from the body a person, Adam — is given a special dignity, but she is declared to be the mother of the living. What a glorious title! Why is Adam not called the father of the living, even though as Eve's husband, he is rightly called the father of Cain? Yet, when she gives birth to her son, she exclaimed: "I have produced a man with the help of the LORD" (Genesis 4:1, NAB). She intuits that it is only when God Himself gives a soul to the newly fertilized egg that a human person has enriched the world.

Note that the serpent, the most astute of all animals, addresses himself to Eve and not to Adam. St. Augustine errs, I believe, in claiming that he does so because "being weaker, she is easier to defeat". Great as he is, there are two things that St. Augustine overlooks: first, that even though Eve is physically weaker, she has an enormous influence on her husband who, as we know, was enchanted when he perceived her. Let me quote Guéranger: "Has the woman, then, no power? She has power, and a great power, —she must address herself to her husband's heart, and gain all by love".[1] This is how Esther conquered King Ahasuerus. Secondly, the wily serpent is a great psychologist. He knew that once seduced, Adam would follow suit. He raised no objection; he followed her lead.

The punishment for both was and is fearful: death. Moreover, Eve was severely punished in the very domain that was her glory—to give life. How illuminating are God's words referring to the enmity that will exist between the serpent and the woman. Why is the male not mentioned? Once again, it is luminous that Eve is the enemy par excellence because being the mother of the living, she is Satan's arch enemy for he was "a murderer from the beginning" and hates life.

But God never abandoned His unfaithful daughters, and in the course of time, created a little girl who from the very moment of her conception was *tota pulchra* (completely beautiful)—a woman whose holy receptivity (*ecce ancilla Domini*—behold the handmaid of the Lord) made her worthy to become the mother of the Savior. A pure lily who, as

---

[1] Prosper Guéranger, *The Liturgical Year: The time after Pentecost*, vol. 1, (Dublin: J. Duffy, 1879), p. 444.

woman, was the mother of the living, and as God's handmaid gave birth to the one who solemnly declared that He is life itself (see John 14:6). From this blessed moment on, the humiliated female was given a model who should make her "humbly proud" that her body has the same pattern as the body of the Blessed one among women.

It is easy to imagine the serpent's rage. Once the female sex was given a glorious model to understand and achieve her mission, he knew that he was heading for a humiliating and crushing defeat. But the intensity of his hatred refused to accept defeat. Alas, after the glorious period of the Middle Ages, when Mary was given the honor which is her due, the poison of secularism was slowly infecting the world. Thanks to the proper "diagnosis" of the unbearable burden of pregnancy and maternity, women are now conscious of the "cause" of their hopeless mediocrity—their budding talents are crushed through their biological make up. They have been told that the moment has come to wake up and escape from the prison of their body and claim their right to abort an unwelcome guest in their womb: abortion is their "birth right."

When a very ill patient is brought to a doctor begging him not only to diagnose his sickness but to offer a possible treatment, the latter will inevitably concentrate his attention on the most serious problem and how this key problem might be responsible for other ailments. We must do the same today as we seek to address the issues of our time. One need not be able to see the future or be a professional pessimist to realize that our contemporary world is at a dangerous crossroad. It should be obvious that "our brave new world" is deadly sick and unless we radically change course we are facing a "sickness unto death." We simply need to recall the changes that have taken place in the course of the last fifty or sixty years. In order to take the pulse of a society, we must look critically at its families, schools, and universities. What is the food that we have been serving children since their grammar school days? One of today's dogmas is that only empirical science and mathematics give us valid knowledge. Metaphysical and ethical ideas are now considered opinions. In a society that proudly declares itself to be democratic, each individual person is entitled to make his own choices and decides what is best for him. In other words, relativism is "democratic," open minded, and proudly declares itself to be disciples of Protagoras who said that, "Man is the measure of all things."

We now operate from the consciousness that we have come of age and can freely decide what is "true" for us. We must recognize the immediate consequence of this appetizing philosophy for all the key questions of human existence such as: Is there a God? Are there moral good and moral evil objective realities or are they just products of a particular society at a particular time in history? We must wake up and realize that if there is no objective truth and anyone's ideas are as good as anyone else's ideas, the very foundations of society are threatened. The natural moral laws, let alone the Ten Commandments, are relegated to the intellectual trash bin so that we are finally "liberated" from the chains that have burdened our ancestors.

Since Genesis, the one deadly enemy of the serpent is the woman because she has been named "mother of the living." This is confirmed by God Himself. Therefore the enemy's most vicious attacks will be directed against her. The whole drama that has been developing in our society over the last sixty years vividly shows how it is through the woman that the enemy is directing his attacks. Feminism was born the day that the enemy convinced some ambitious women that they will never achieve greatness unless they liberate themselves from the burden to give birth that was so unfairly placed on their shoulders. He convinced them to believe maternity is a jail and it is high time that women free themselves from these unbearable chains. It is only natural that the contraceptive mentality embraced in the sixties was seen as a key instrument in freeing women from this unfair burden. Yet, we cannot escape the individual and societal consequences of contraception predicted by Pope Paul VI in *Humanae Vitae* in 1968—lower moral standards, greater infidelity, less respect for women by men, and coercive use of reproductive technology by governments—all evident today. This was followed by the legalization of abortion which should be understood in all its gravity as the ultimate violation of woman with immeasurable societal implications. The continued rejection of natural law and the radical redefinition of what it means to be a woman and a man will bring even more grave consequences.

We must find ways to strengthen our Christian families, show the complementarity and equal dignity of masculinity and femininity, and become lights in a world so darkened by the lies of the enemy. In a particular way, it is through the "mother of the living" that these lies must be rejected because *"God entrusts the human being to her in a special way."*[2] The woman must recognize her key role in the family and society, which is the heart of a nation and all of humanity. Indeed, once again, it us urgent for women to realize that "it is a privilege to be one" and to embrace all the responsibilities and blessings that come with being a woman.

—ALICE VON HILDEBRAND
August 22, 2015
*Feast of the Queenship
of the Blessed Virgin Mary*

---

[2] John Paul II, *Mulieris Dignitatem* (August 15, 1989), 30 (emphasis in original).

PART I
Arguments Against the Privilege of Being a Woman

SECULAR ARGUMENTS

How can it be a privilege for a woman to be called "the second sex" (*sexus sequior*); to be considered less talented, less strong, less creative, less interesting, less intelligent, less artistic than her male counterpart?

All great creations of mankind have been made by men: in architecture, in fine arts, in theology, in philosophy, in science, in technology. The history of the world is mostly the history of the achievements of human males; from time to time, a female is mentioned, but she is then commended for her "manly" qualities, or for having "a virile mind."[1] Simone de Beauvoir and Simone Weil are frequently praised for this same reason. On the other hand, we look down upon someone who is designated as "effeminate" or "womanish."

According to statistics, most people prefer to have a boy baby than to have a girl. This is true not only in societies like China, where traditionally girls have been abandoned and even murdered. Today one million six hundred thousand baby girls are abandoned.[2] More female than male babies are aborted. Not long ago, the *New York Times* reported that in Korea women feel guilty toward their husbands when they produce "only" girls. They do not seem to know that, biologically speaking, it is the male who determines the sex of the child!

Who would choose to have a body which, from the time of puberty on, can be burdensome, can cause discomfort and even severe pain? Who would choose to be nauseated for weeks, and sometimes months, during pregnancy? Who would choose to give birth in agonizing pain? When the Old Testament wishes to illustrate severe trials, it usually refers to a woman in labor.[3]

Men want women to exist, but they do not want to be women themselves.[4] Simone de Beauvoir writes that "…men are human beings; women are just females."[5] She claims that women cannot transcend, and that they "produce nothing."[6] Women are "pure objects" who exist in order to satisfy the cravings of the male sex. According to her, women are "disgusted by their own sex."[7] They loathe being women. This is what G. K. Chesterton had in mind when he wrote that a feminist is someone who "dislikes the chief feminine characteristics."[8] As a result, the agenda of feminists, while animated by a hatred of men, aims at virilizing women so that they can gain control over their bodies, their destiny. Once liberated from biological ties, women will be able to develop their talents which, for centuries, have been crushed by social taboos. According to de Beauvoir, the scarcity of female accomplishments is to be explained "by the general mediocrity of their situation...."[9]

The leading feminists encourage their disciples to become masters of their destiny instead of being subject to a quirk of nature. They must liberate themselves and become "free." In order to achieve this aim, feminists proclaim the identity of men and women. The wiser Chesterton wrote, "There is nothing so certain to lead to inequality as identity."[10]

Bluntly speaking, women have traditionally been considered "inferior" to men. This is the dictate of nature: "Anatomy is destiny."[11] To plead their cause, feminist scholars have been efficient at unearthing nasty things that men have said or written about women. That many famous men have spoken disparagingly of women cannot be denied. Aristotle refers to females as "deficient males."[12] In the Old Testament there are numerous statements about women that are far from complimentary. Some deserve to be quoted: "Any wickedness but not the wickedness of a wife."[13] "I would rather dwell with a lion and a dragon than dwell with an evil wife."[14] "From a woman sin had its beginning, and because of her we all die."[15] "An evil wife is an ox yoke which chafes; taking hold of her is like grasping a scorpion."[16] "It is a woman who brings shame and disgrace."[17] "One man among a thousand I found, but a woman among all these I have not found."[18] "A man who wishes you ill is better than a woman who wishes you well."[19]

The Torah does not speak favorably of a woman's intellect: "Rather burn Torah than try to explain it to a woman."[20] Some Fathers of the Church follow suit. The great Saint John Chrysostom wrote: "Among all wild beasts, there is none to be found which is more harmful than the woman."[21] According to Luther, the meaning of a woman's life is to procreate: "the work and word of God tell us clearly that women must be used for marriage or for prostitution. If women get tired and die of bearing, there is no harm in that: let them die so long as they bear: they are made for that."[22]

The secularist view is hardly more flattering. In *Hamlet*, William Shakespeare wrote the often-quoted words: "Frailty, thy name is woman."[23] John Milton writes that "the woman is a pretty mistake."[24] (What should be said, we might ask, of a woman who is not pretty?) Kant—in one of his "humble" moods—writes that "the woman is less talented, morally inferior to man."[25] With Teutonic brutality Friedrich Nietzsche writes, "When you go to a woman, do not forget your whip."[26] Arthur

Schopenhauer speaks of women with contempt: "Women are childish, frivolous and short-sighted...big children all their life long."[27] With sarcasm and wit, he gives vent to his intense dislike of his mother. His essay on women is a long litany of negative female attributes. Not only does he despise a woman's intellect, but he even objects to calling women "the fair sex." According to him, women are "the unaesthetic sex."[28]

Alexandre Dumas writes that "According to the Bible, woman was the last thing God made. It must have been a Saturday [sic] night: clearly he was tired."[29] Lord Byron laments the fact that whereas men cannot stand women, they cannot live without them.[30] A German thinker, today totally forgotten, by the name of Weininger, made headlines by writing that "women's minds are pure nonsense."[31] His book was reprinted twenty-five times. Sigmund Freud made the interesting "scientific" discovery that every little girl is born with "penis envy," which is long before she could possibly know that this organ exists.

Yet feminists carefully refrain from mentioning the beautiful statements that men have made throughout history such as "she [a good wife] is far more precious than jewels;"[32] or "do not deprive yourself of a wise and good wife; for her charm is worth more than gold."[33] Dante sings the praise of the *donna angelicata* (woman viewed as an angel). He immortalized Beatrice, his one great love, whose personality is a light and an inspiration in the poet's life, and whose mission is to lead him to God. Shakespeare's female characters are often sublime. Lamartine refers to women as *"anges mortels, création divine"* ("mortal angels, divine creation"). Schiller rhapsodizes about the female sex.[34] Theodor Haecker claims that nature made woman more perfect than man because she is more inclined to love and to give herself.[35] The noblest characters in Claudel's plays are women (e.g., Violaine, Sygne). Forced to face this truth, de Beauvoir interprets it in her feminist way. She writes: "But if his women [Claudel's] are thus remarkably devoted to the heroism of sanctity, it is above all because Claudel still views them in a masculine perspective."[36] As sanctity is devalued in de Beauvoir's eyes (as a poor substitute for great achievements), the highest praise that can be given anyone male or female — namely holiness — is, to her mind, only a left-handed compliment.

That such divergent statements can be made about women can find sundry explanations. It is usually true that an impure man, or one hooked on pornography, will look down upon women. On the other hand, a man steeped in the supernatural will look up to the sex that was honored to give birth to the Savior of the world. In the end, unwarranted generalizations are typical of shallow minds. That some women are "big children their whole life long," that some women are refinedly wicked, that some are stupid, and so on are as dull as statements claiming that some men are bestial, some are brutal, some are stupid (because stupidity, against which the gods themselves fight in vain, is pretty fairly distributed between the two sexes).

But the negative statements made about the "weaker sex"—highlighted and endlessly repeated by feminists—have gained currency and are the water driving their mill. Such words are no doubt partially responsible for this revolutionary movement that has gained so much impetus in the contemporary world.

According to feminists, under societal pressure women have for centuries accepted their "inferiority," and in many countries they still do. But now, in "developed nations," the *kairos* is ripe (the time is ripe) for a reassessment of this humiliating situation. Aware of the injustice that they have been subjected to, feminists now claim their right to equal footing with the male sex. This aim is supposedly to be achieved by competing with men in the work force, instead of being exiled in *Kirche, Kueche, and Kinder* (the three K's of the German language: church, kitchen, and children). According to de Beauvoir, liberation from the menial tasks of the home is the great noble achievement of socialism (by which she means Soviet Russia).[37] She writes, "…the fate of woman and that of socialism are intimately bound…."[38] This claim is hotly contested by contemporary Russian author Tatiana Goricheva. Speaking about the situation of women in Soviet Russia, she writes: "And women among us suffer twice if not three times as much as men."[39]

That some women have been abominably treated by some men cannot and should not be denied. Kierkegaard writes, "What abominations has the world not seen in the relationship between man and woman—that she, almost like an animal, was a despised creature compared to the male, a creature of another species."[40] Chesterton too admits this fact: "I do not deny that women have been wronged and even tortured; but I doubt if they were ever tortured so much as they are tortured now by the absurd modern attempt to make them domestic empresses and competitive clerks at the same time." The solution he offers is "…to destroy the tyranny. They [the feminists] want to destroy the womanhood."[41]

The abuse that many women have been subjected to has often been illustrated in literature: Let us recall the brutal treatment that the crippled sister of Lebyadkin, in Dostoevsky's *The Possessed*, is subjected to by her ruthless and mostly drunk brother. Obviously the great Russian writer was referring to real facts. This sad story has often been true in the past and is still true today. That male chauvinism is nothing but a combination of childish male pride and brutality cannot be contested. Yet it seems evident that even in the face of their physical vulnerability, given their greater sensitivity, their more subtle intuitions, their talent for feeling themselves into others, women have greater possibilities of uplifting or of hurting others than those usually granted to the opposite sex.

It is noteworthy that in Sirach, the author is eloquent in speaking about the wickedness that wives may possess since original sin, but no mention is made of the brutality, selfishness, and hardness of heart of some husbands. The author probably wished to draw our attention to the fact that when women are wicked and choose to tread on what Søren Kierkegaard calls "the path of perdition," they often surpass the wickedness of their male counterpart. La Bruyère writes, "Women are all in extremes, either better or worse than men."[42] Kierkegaard defends the same thesis: "...it belongs to her nature to be more perfect and more imperfect than man. If one would indicate the purest and most perfect quality, one says, 'a woman'; if one would indicate the weakest, the most feeble thing, one says 'a woman'; if one would give a notion of a spiritual quality raised above all sensuousness, one says 'a woman'; if one would give a notion of the sensuous, one says 'a woman'; if one would indicate innocence in all its lofty greatness, one says 'a woman'; if one would point to the depressing feeling of sin, one says 'a woman.' In a certain sense, therefore, woman is more perfect than man...."[43] Nietzsche follows suit: *"das vollkommene Weib ist ein hoeherer typus als der vollkommene Mann"* ("the perfect woman stands higher than a perfect man").[44] But he also writes that *"das Weib ist unsaeglich viel boeser als der Mann"* ("woman is much more wicked than man").[45]

But is the feminist response to these inequalities and injustices a solution which will benefit the Church, society at large, marriage, the family, and women themselves? Unwittingly, the feminists acknowledge the superiority of the male sex by wishing to become like men. They foolishly want to alter inequality rather than to achieve truth or justice. Femininity is a linchpin of human life; once it is uprooted, the consequences are disastrous. In fact, experience proves that feminism benefits men and harms women.[46]

Man, being free, is able to give an appropriate response to every situation; he is equally free to give a wrong response. Human nature being wounded by original sin, men are more prone to give wrong responses than valid ones. Whereas we can sin without anyone's help, we cannot do good without God's grace, for which we must humbly pray. This is something that many fail to do.

CHRISTIANITY AND ARGUMENTS AGAINST THE PRIVILEGE

It was de Beauvoir's belief that the Bible and, particularly, Christian ideology carry a heavy responsibility for the deplorable and humiliating situation that women find themselves in.[47] According to her reading, from Genesis on, woman has been declared to be man's servant. She should be obedient, submissive, and accept her inferiority without revolt. To be in a subordinate position is God's will for her. This is how she will achieve salvation. She will be exalted to the extent that she acknowledges and accepts her servitude. Adam was created before Eve. To de Beauvoir, this signifies that she was an afterthought. She was formed from Adam's rib and was created to supply companionship to someone who was feeling hopelessly lonesome.

She was the one who yielded to the serpent's crafty promise; she was the one who gave the forbidden fruit to her husband and thereby caused his ruin and ours. Although both culprits were severely punished, by loss of the life of grace, by loss of preternatural gifts that had been granted to them—including immortality of the body, freedom from sickness and pain—she was more severely chastised than her husband. True, he was condemned to earn his bread with the sweat of his brow (a punishment which millions of women share with men), but she was punished in the very sphere that was her glory—maternity. From now on, she was condemned to give birth in pain and anguish. Moreover, she was declared to be "subject to her husband." Her status of inferiority was sealed.

According to de Beauvoir, this inferiority is confirmed in the New Testament. Has not Mary declared herself to be "the handmaid of the Lord?" She writes, "As servant, woman is entitled to the most splendid deification."[48] Mary is praised for her obedience and submission. She is rewarded with becoming the mother of the Savior by declaring herself to be "the handmaid of the Lord." According to the French feminist, her final defeat is sealed when, after giving birth to a male child, she kneels in front of Him and adores Him. This act of adoration constitutes the "ultimate male victory."[49] De Beauvoir takes the freedom of making this kneeling addition to Saint Luke's Gospel. The Evangelist only tells us that she "…wrapped Him in swaddling cloths, and put Him in a manger…."[50] Moreover, the French feminist "forgets" to mention that Saint Paul tells us that *all* knees should bend in front of the Savior and, as knees have no sex, men are definitely included.[51] The humble shepherds were then informed that "…to you is born this day in the city of David, a Saviour…."[52] These simple men hastened to give homage to the Newborn King. The aristocratic Magi followed suit and Saint Matthew informs us that "…they fell down and worshiped Him."[53] She also forgets that if all knees should bend in front of the Savior, all heads should bow in front of His mother.[54]

The feminists' reading of the Bible is inevitably thwarted by their philosophy; in fact, they are rewriting this inspired book according to their own subjective "inspiration." In the long run, it leads them paradoxically to place women at the apex of creation and to proclaim the superiority of the female sex. God becomes a She, and Christ will be rebaptized Christa! With a secularistic view, the war between the sexes is inevitable.

 PART II
Arguments for the Privilege
of Being a Woman

THE SUPERNATURAL VIEW

In order to understand the greatness of a woman's mission, we must open our minds and hearts to the message of the supernatural. It is the key that will reveal to us the greatness of femininity. It is one thing to read a text; it is another to interpret it correctly. All the arguments which seem to favor the thesis that the Bible has been discriminating against women from the very beginning can easily be reversed by interpreting the sacred text with the eyes of faith.

That men and women are perfectly equal in dignity—both being made to God's image and likeness—cannot be contested. But to be created last does not indicate inferiority. As a matter of fact, it could be argued that there is an ascending line in creation: from inanimate matter, to plants, lower animals, mammals, man, and finally, woman. Obviously we are not inferring that woman, being created last, is superior to man. We only wish to show that the argument used to prove her "inferiority" is not valid and can be turned on its head.

The fact that Eve's body was fashioned from Adam's rib can also easily be interpreted as a sign of special dignity and preciousness: for to be made from the body of a human person (made in God's image and likeness) is definitely nobler than being fashioned from the dust of the earth.

Indeed, the punishment meted out to Eve, as de Beauvoir points out, was particularly severe. As mentioned above, when referring to excruciating pains, the Old Testament mentions the pangs of childbirth. But, in the light of redemption (which has given a sublime meaning to suffering), to suffer agony to bring another human being into the world is a premonition of the sufferings of Christ whose blood has redeemed us. It intimates that if Eve carries a heavy responsibility for the tragedy of original sin, the new Eve will play a cardinal role in the work of redemption. Saint Andrew of Crete writes: "The women applaud, for if at another time it was a woman who was the imprudent occasion of sin, now too it is a woman who brings in the first fruits of salvation."[55] Kierkegaard writes: "it is my conviction that if it was a woman that ruined man, it was woman also that has fairly and honestly made reparation and still does so...."[56] More will be said about this later.

The New Testament highlights magnificently the glorious role assigned to women. At the Annunciation, the Angel Gabriel addresses himself to a young virgin betrothed to Joseph. She is offered the overwhelming privilege of being overshadowed by the Holy Spirit and becoming the mother of the Savior. She declares herself to be the handmaid of the Lord and conceives the Holy One. *Saint Joseph is neither present nor even informed* of the amazing miracle which has taken place in the one he loves. The humble Virgin of Nazareth is alone in center stage. It is only when he notices that she is with child that he is informed, in a dream, of the mystery that has taken place in the Virgin Mary's womb. The Gospel is silent about the sufferings that Mary must have undergone until Joseph was informed that he was betrothed to the most blessed of all women. Faith and an immense confidence in God must have sustained them both during this trial. Revelation limits itself to telling us what we need for Salvation; many sacred mysteries are left in the dark. It is only in Eternity that we shall be privileged to contemplate the fullness of God's loving plans.

If we are to speak of Church practices, it is not by accident that seven of the fifteen decades of the rosary are dedicated to Mary, once again putting the limelight on her unique role in the economy of redemption. Moreover, the Stations of the Cross honor women. The fourth station pictures the Savior meeting His beloved mother; not a word is said about this heartbreaking encounter, but the faithful are challenged to meditate reverently upon this scene of ultimate love and ultimate sorrow which renders words meaningless. Simon of Cyrene did indeed help carry Christ's cross, but Saint Luke tells us explicitly that "he was forced" to do so.[57] The holy women certainly envied Him: How *they* would have welcomed the possibility of partaking physically in the sufferings of the one they loved so ardently. Veronica piously wipes her Savior's face. The women of Jerusalem weep over the fate of the Holy One unjustly condemned to death while the soldiers brutally mistreat Him. The holy women are all assembled at the foot of the cross. No woman was privileged to see Christ transfigured on Mount Tabor, but they were there at the Crucifixion. This is — once again — deeply meaningful: They were not given to see Him transfigured; but they were permitted to see Him "bruised for our iniquities, smitten by God and afflicted."[58] The apostles had fled. Saint John — the disciple Jesus loved — did come back; and it was to him that the dying Savior confided His mother with the words: "This is your mother."

The first witness of the resurrection was a woman: Mary Magdalen. Typically enough, the apostles refused to believe her testimony, making the foolish remark that "it was just woman's talk." She knew that she had been privileged to see the risen Lord and did not try to justify herself. She knew the One she loved would defend her by appearing to those whose faith had faltered. One likes to think that the apostles later apologized to Mary Magdalen for rejecting her testimony, but Holy Scripture is silent on this point; there are secrets that will only be revealed in eternity. She certainly did not ask for apologies (a true Christian never solicits them), when her heart was overflowing with the joy that "He has risen from the dead," never to die again. She knew He was the conqueror of death, now a triumphant victor. Mary Magdalen believed more strongly because she loved more.

In the *Apocalypse*, once again, the role of women in the New Testament is gloriously highlighted. Saint John was granted a vision of a woman as bright as the sun, crowned with stars. Mysterious as this sacred writing is, once again we are given a chance to see how grossly unfair and utterly unscholarly it is to accuse Christianity of having denigrated women and assigned to them an insignificant role.

As soon as we abandon a secularistic interpretation of the Bible, we can perceive that, from a supernatural point of view, *women are actually granted a privileged position* in the economy of redemption. Those who persist in wearing secularistic lenses have eyes and do not see, have ears and do not hear. For the Bible cannot be understood except in an attitude of humble receptivity, that is, "on one's knees," (as Kierkegaard puts it). So-called "biblical" scholars may know Aramaic and Greek but nevertheless radically misunderstand the divine message, because their "scholarship" has warped their faith. A tacit refusal to receive God's message—because of intellectual pride—is punished by blindness.

Granted that women have often been denigrated, humiliated, and looked down upon in the course of human history, we must keep in mind that the culprits are always *individual* men, tainted by original sin and anxious to place themselves above others, often in order to compensate for their own mediocrity.[59] One thing is certain: The Catholic Church, she who has elevated women to an extraordinary dignity, is and always has been a convenient scapegoat. It is psychologically so satisfying to find an institution to blame for all the evils afflicting the world, while the accuser wraps himself comfortably in the mantle of blamelessness! Ignorant people stubbornly refuse to make a distinction between Her Holiness as Bride of Christ and Holy Teacher and the often pitiful actions of her wayward and rebellious children. The Church grants all her children the means of achieving holiness—*but she cannot force them to become holy.* It is noteworthy that the Church is at times censured for abusing her authority by "imposing" her dogmatic and moral teaching on her children, without consulting them! But the next moment, her accusers criticize her for not using her authority to force her children to live according to the Gospel.[60]

The denigration of women is clearly a sad consequence of original sin *which has subverted the hierarchy of values.* By wishing to "become equal to God" (without God), Adam and Eve were, in fact, revolting against their creaturehood, that is, their total dependence upon God. He was the creator; they were His subjects. Original sin was a sin of pride, of disobedience, of irreverence, and of metaphysical revolt that led to an inversion of the hierarchy of values.

By arrogantly declaring themselves equal to God, Adam and Eve were waging war on this hierarchy. And once this equilibrium was broken, it brought in its train a whole series of disastrous consequences, *particularly ominous for women.* Just as our parents' souls revolted against God, their bodies revolted against their souls, to which they had been subject. And they realized "that they were naked." In other words—and this has been beautifully commented upon by our Holy Father—lust made its entrance into the world and waged war against spousal love which, up to that tragic moment, had been the glorious theme and the backbone of the relationship between our first parents: a tender affection finding its expression in the marital embrace.

PART III

From Paganism to Modern Values: Denigration of Woman

The world in which we now live is a world whose outlook is so distorted that we absolutize what is relative (money-making, power, success) and relativize what is absolute (truth, moral values, and God).[61] Power, riches, fame, success, and dominance are idolized; humility, chastity, modesty, self-sacrifice, and service are looked down upon as signs of weakness. This last sentence, Nietzsche's philosophy in a nutshell—the glorification of strength and the denigration of weakness—has become the shallow core of modern thought and feminist belief.

The gravity of their offense was such that it was impossible for our first parents to recover the priceless gift of supernatural life. God alone could do so and, in His infinite mercy and goodness, He chose to send us His only Son to effect our redemption by His death at Calvary. As every sin brings with it its own punishment, is it surprising that today we have become so morally blind (for wickedness blinds) that we save baby whales at great cost, and murder millions of unborn children?[62]

Man's conscience has been so *darkened* by his repeated infidelities toward God that these outrageous murders are no longer registered as being crimes that cry to heaven. Baby murderers go to bed with a good conscience and the satisfaction of having been "efficient." Bernard Nathanson, in his gripping work *The Hand of God*, relates that after having performed an abortion he had the pleasant feeling of having completed a work well done and of having "liberated" pregnant women from a burden hateful to them. Babies are cheap to make. Baby whales are more costly.

Our first parents' minds were darkened by sin, their wills were weakened, their judgment became distorted. The hierarchy of values being upset, *male accomplishments became overvalued.* Physical strength became glorified and weakness was looked down upon as a proof of inferiority. This is written in the book of Wisdom, referring to the language of the ungodly: "but let our might be our law of right, for what is weak proves itself to be useless."[63]

Homer's *Iliad* illustrates this. The Greek heroes are strong, healthy, victorious. Those who are conquered and defeated deserve to become slaves; they are plainly inferior. It is noteworthy that the greatest cultures have often been defeated by primitive tribes that had little or no culture, but plenty of physical daring and stamina.[64] Hand in hand with the overestimation of strength and virility goes an overestimation of accomplishments, feats, performances, success. In our society to be a "self-made man" calls for awe. A Bill Gates, an Oprah Winfrey, or even a Bill Clinton inspire people with a totally illegitimate feeling of admiration. But success does not guarantee authentic greatness. Many scoundrels have been incredibly successful, too successful for their own good. Original sin blinds us to the fact that all these feats, often aided by ruthlessness, craftiness, or even plain luck, have no value in the light of eternity. We should always raise the question: *Quid est hoc ad aeternitatem?* (What is this in light of eternity?). In fact, it is only dust and ashes. No one enters the gates of heaven because he is a millionaire; no one is worthy to see God because he is "famous." Indeed, worldly "wisdom" is sheer foolishness. This has been seen by Socrates, and emphatically repeated by Saint Paul, "for the foolishness of God is wiser than men, and the weakness of God is stronger than men."[65] Against the background of the supernatural, the inanity of human praise becomes evident.

A further consequence of this broken equilibrium is that we tend to overrate "creativity." To be successful in our contemporary world, one must be "inventive." Creativity does have a positive ring, but the crucial question is not whether a person is "creative," but rather "what does he create?" To praise an innovative type of architecture without asking whether or not it is beautiful is inane. To honor someone because of the number of books and articles he has published without investigating whether or not they are true is once again to be off-track. The lopsided view which today has gained currency inevitably leads feminists to overrate "creativity," "novelty," and "fashion," changes sought for their own sake; these tickle people's curiosity and draw them into the vortex of total metaphysical instability. It is another way of drawing attention away from "eternal truths" and unchanging values.

The spirit of the time teaches us that today everything depends upon what is "in the air," what people want. In this spiritual climate, tradition is doomed. The past is looked down upon as "dead," as having nothing to give to "modern man."[66] As women are weaker than men, and as they do not bask in the limelight as much as men do, as they are less "creative" than the strong sex, they are bound to be the victims of this distorted hierarchy of values. That women have been victimized by this distortion of the hierarchy of values is deplorable and sad indeed; *but that feminists have endorsed this inversion is still more pitiful.* Imprisoned in the spiritual jail of secular categories, they fail to understand *that their true mission is to swim against the tide* and, with God's grace, help restore the proper hierarchy of values.

By living up to their calling, women will succeed in guaranteeing a proper recognition of the unique value of femininity and its crucial mission in the world. This is proved by innumerable testimonies. A French writer by the name of Vinet wrote that "the value of a people is to be gauged by the value of its women" (*"un peuple vaut ce que valent ses femmes"*).[67] Strong men are often cowed by women, particularly by their wives. In his life of Gandhi, Louis Fisher writes, "Gandhi feared neither man nor government, neither prison, nor poverty nor death. But he did fear his wife."[68] In the same book, referring to the conflict that developed between India and Pakistan, he writes, "Moslem women are the real force behind their men."[69] The fear that wives can inspire in their husbands is also stressed in Michael Scammell's life of Solzhenitsyn. He writes, "Seemingly all-powerful in his confrontation with the Soviet government…he was yet helpless when faced with the wrath of a discarded woman."[70] In her book *Catherine the Great,* Joan Haslip writes that "he [Stanislaus] was at his happiest with the feminine members of his court, for the women were far cleverer and better educated. Visitors to Poland were always impressed by the obvious superiority of women and their interest in politics and the arts."[71] In her book on Adolf von Hildebrand, Isolde Kurz relates that the artist's wife, Irene, told her that since the death of Fieldler, the friendships that her husband valued most were those he had with women."[72] In his memoirs, *Erlebte Weltgeschichte*, the famous educator F. W. Foerster makes the claim that in France women are definitely "the strong sex."[73] Pearl Buck writes that in China "it was true that generally speaking the men were inferior to the women, and this I suppose was because boys were so spoiled in Chinese homes...the Chinese woman usually emerges the stronger character...."[74] She also cites the words of Confucius, "Where the woman is faithful, no evil can befall. The woman is the root and the man the tree. The tree grows only as high as the root is strong,"[75] and further, "The strongest thing on earth is a woman...."[76] Albert Speer, the personal architect of Adolf Hitler, writes in his memoirs that "in general the wives of the regime's bigwigs resisted the temptation of power far more than their husbands...they looked at the often grotesque antics of their husbands with inner reservation...."[77] Obviously the strength that these men note in women refers not to exterior accomplishments *but to the moral power* that a woman can possess.

These accolades indicate clearly that the "weakness" of the female sex, as far as accomplishments and productivity are concerned, can be more than compensated by her moral strength *when she lives up to her calling.* That is, when she loves. The influence that she can exercise over her male partner is great indeed when it manifests itself not by issuing commands but by example and gentle persuasion. On the other hand, when she betrays her mission, she can indeed be man's downfall. Her role is a key one. Kierkegaard wrote that "woman is the conscience of man."[78] But her conscience must be illumined by faith and enlivened by true love; it must not be a conscience distorted by self-centered relativism.

But feminists — blinded by secularism — do what, in fact, will lead to a worsening of women's situation. *Feminists are women's great enemy.* Not only will they not succeed in trying to become like men, but they will also inevitably jeopardize the sublime mission confided to them. Kierkegaard writes, "I hate all talk about the emancipation of woman. God forbid that it may ever come to pass. I cannot tell you with what pain this thought is able to pierce my heart, nor what passionate exasperation, what hate I feel toward every one who gives vent to such talk. It is my comfort that those who proclaim such wisdom are not as wise as serpents but are for the most part blockheads whose nonsense can do no harm.... no base seducer could think out a more dangerous doctrine for woman, for once he has made her believe this she is entirely in his power, at the mercy of his will, she can be nothing for him except a prey to his whims, whereas as woman, she can be everything for him."[79] Nietzsche perceived clearly that the emancipation of women is a symptom that their feminine instincts are weakening.[80] He stresses that this "emancipation" in fact means the "masculinization" of women.[81]

The whole tragedy of contemporary feminism — which Cardinal Josef Ratzinger considers one of the greatest threats menacing the Church — stems from a lack of faith and a loss of the sense of the supernatural. Feminism is inconceivable in a world rooted in Judeo-Christian values. But it is in the New Testament that the full glory of the female mission and vocation shines in the person of the Holy Virgin of Nazareth who accepted to become the mother of the Redeemer while remaining a virgin (as prophesied by Isaiah). Once spiritual eyesight, severely distorted by original sin, has been corrected by the lenses of faith, we are in a position to understand God's creation as He meant it to be and to reject with horror the view offered by the deforming lenses of secularism.

Yet we live in a world so deeply steeped in secularism that many of us are not even aware that we are influenced by its disastrous ideology. There are some devout and faithful Christians who would be offended if accused of being tainted by the spirit of the time (or Zeitgeist), but nevertheless — in certain concrete situations—their attitude betrays that the fumes of secularism have penetrated into their spiritual lungs and, rising to their brains, have colored their judgment. It is only by being aware of the danger of the Zeitgeist, and daily purging ourselves of its disastrous influence, that we can hope to be freed from its subtle poison. In his *Memoirs*, my husband repeatedly underlines the fact that many faithful, sincere Catholics were infected by the poison of Nazism without being aware of it.

One further deplorable consequence of this secularistic view is the claim that "service is degrading."[82] It is viewed as antidemocratic. It is humiliating. Humility is a virtue that finds little favor in the secularistic world. It is only puzzled and confused by the words of Psalm 118:71: "it is good for me that I was humbled that I might learn your statutes." Once again, this error inevitably leads to a denigration of women whose mission traditionally has been to serve—following thereby our Lord who said, "I have not come to be served but to serve."[83] How can anyone meditating on these words come to the conclusion that to serve, which is a form of love, is degrading? The most glorious title of the Holy Father was introduced by Gregory VII who called him *servus servorum Dei* (the servant of the servants of God), for authority is given to the pope, not for his personal advantage, but for the benefit of those confided to his care. Woe to the pontiff who abuses this authority and basks in the power given him. Woe to him whose ambition has been the *leitmotiv* of his ascension to the pontifical throne. Those worthy of this honor are those who do not seek it, do not even desire it.[84] What characterizes holiness is this limitless readiness to serve others. In his book *Saint Bernard*, Ratisbonne writes, "the humble Bernard, remained inflexibly on the lowest step; nor would he ever exchange for any worldly advantage the privilege of being the servant of the least of his brethren."[85]

The new age philosophy of feminism, in waging war on femininity, is in fact waging war on Christianity. For in the divine plan both are intimately linked. Not socialism, as Simone de Beauvoir believed, but Christ is the great ally of women. Modern ideology wages war on the Gospel which teaches humility and that those who lower themselves will be exalted. Indeed, there can be no reconciliation between an ideology that advocates power and success and the one whose core demonstrates that the way to God is the humble acceptance of one's helplessness: "Come to my aid, O Lord, hasten to help me." Both the Old and the New Testaments condemn pride, arrogance, self-assurance, and the stupidity of those who believe that they do not need God. The cry of every Christian, echoing Saint Peter sinking in the sea of Galilee, is "Help me, O Lord, lest I perish."

Christianity teaches that exterior feats (the invention of computers, of the atomic bomb, or landing on the moon) are dust and ashes in God's sight. We shall be judged not according to our "performance" in the secular world, but according to our humility and charity. It is wise to remember that the world will perish by fire which will destroy all things.[86] It is quite conceivable that the mind-boggling technological progress of the last sixty years, if severed from wisdom, will bring about man's downfall. Plato wrote centuries ago, in the first book of *The Laws*, that man is his own worst enemy. It was true then; it is true today. Man can now destroy the world by his own mere "fiat"—his diabolical caricature of God's creation. One thing is certain: When the time has come, nothing which is man-made will subsist. One day, all human accomplishments will be reduced to a pile of ashes. But every single child to whom a woman has given birth will live forever, for he has been given an immortal soul made to God's image and likeness. In this light, the assertion of de Beauvoir that "women produce nothing" becomes particularly ludicrous.[87]

PART IV
Woman: The Privileged Sex

As mentioned above, feminists resent the fact that several great Christian thinkers, beginning with Saint Peter, have referred to women as being "the weaker sex."[88] Several Fathers of the Church followed suit. Obviously these pillars of Christianity have something valid in mind. It would be unwise on our part to discard it outright as an expression of "male chauvinism."

What can be meant by "weaker?" An obvious answer would be that the "fair sex" is physically weaker than its male counterpart. This is something so obvious that we can ignore this explanation as irrelevant. Moreover, there would be no reason for the most "sensitive" feminist to be offended for it is an undeniable fact. But the feminists are offended because they assume that "weaker" means less intelligent, less talented, less reliable, less moral, etc. As we saw, numerous male sayings support this thesis. It is true that the word "weak" is often used to refer to things, actions, or attitudes which are flawed. One speaks of a "weak argument," a "weak defense," a "weak character," "weak health," a "weak performance." In all these cases, weakness refers to something defective and unsatisfactory. As we saw, Greek literature (I am thinking of Homer) glorified strength, accomplishment, courage, and power. The weak one is defeated, flouted, and ridiculed. Our contemporary idolization of sports stems from the same root. He who wins is a hero; this is how President Bush qualified the Americans who won a gold medal at the Olympic games in Seoul! He who is defeated is a weakling. The Belgian football team defeated in Paris in June 1998 was a case in point. Hecklers greeted them when they returned to Brussels.

CONS AND PROS OF WEAKNESS

Cons

"Weak" can refer to what is fragile, delicate, breakable, vulnerable, sensitive. Women are more vulnerable than men and this vulnerability can render them helpless and irritable. They are usually less capable than men to fend for themselves. How often the Bible reminds us of the duty to care for widows. Widowers are not mentioned.

That women are in this sense weaker than men is exemplified by female tears. If all the tears shed by women had been collected since the beginning of the world, they would compete with the sea. The tears shed by men might fill a pond of modest size. Not only do they cry much more than men, but moreover, they are not ashamed of their tears, whereas there are men who would rather die than be tearful. More will be said about this later.

Because of "the meld of heart and mind" which characterizes women,[89] they are more likely to be wounded than men, whose power of abstraction often shields them from negative feelings. Women have much less control over their emotions; they usually have greater sensitivity, they are more intuitive. Their bodies are mirrors of their psyche and seem to be more closely connected than in men. This innate trait—when not properly guided—may lead them to yield to seduction and to some serious moral weaknesses, for example, partisanship, subjectivism in judging situations and persons. More than men, women are likely to be attracted by magic.[90] This may take the form of spiritism, tarot cards, or Ouija boards. Fortune-tellers are often women.

This might be another point Saint Peter and Saint Augustine had in mind when they called women "the weaker sex." Women take their feelings much more seriously than men do, and so they have a tendency to dwell upon them and fall into self-centeredness. They are more likely than men to be romantic and sentimental (let us think of

Madame Bovary), to become prey to an unhealthy exaltation, to escape into the world of their dreams, and to be dominated by their imagination and their fancy. Throughout her autobiography, Saint Teresa of Avila repeatedly refers to the dangers menacing the spiritual life of "the weak sex": emotionalism, dreaming, illusions, self-centeredness. She repeatedly stresses how much they are in need of guidance. Two great spiritual directors, Saint Francis of Sales and Dom Colomba Marmion, emphasize the fact that "however intellectual or enlightened a woman may be, God, according to the ordinary rulings of His providence, wills her to be directed by a man who is His minister."[91] This is a theme which keeps recurring in his spiritual letters. Women need men whose mission is to help them to channel their emotions, *to distinguish between those that are valid and those that are tainted by irrationality*, those which are legitimate and those which are illegitimate.

But Saint Teresa—echoing Saint Peter Alcantara—also writes that more women than men receive extraordinary graces, that they are more receptive to God's voice and particularly capable of heroic donation when their heart is purified.[92] The more privileged they are, the more they need guidance. Saint Teresa had the wisdom of always turning to wise and holy spiritual directors to help her discern the validity of her mystical experiences.

Without such guidance or grace woman may be weak enough to misuse one of her great gifts, her beauty, to her own destruction and that of others. The prostitute (the most tragic of women) has mastered the sad art of seduction. She knows which buttons to press to catch a client. Since original sin, lust has entered into the human heart and, unless a person is protected by grace and a faithful life of prayer, it is, alas, true that most human beings will fall into the nets of coarse sexual attraction. What is so tragic about this is that the beauty of the divine plan for the relations between men and women is thereby trampled upon and badly stained. It is indeed a shameful thing to use and abuse another human being. Moreover, sexual sins disgrace man's soul in a way that cannot be understood when our conception of this mysterious sphere is purely biological. On the other hand, it is inconceivable for anyone to fall into sexual depravity (another word for filth) if he remains aware that God sees him at all times. There are deeds that can only be accomplished in darkness.

The master psychologist Dostoevsky has powerfully depicted in *The Brothers Karamazov* how an unfortunate woman called Gruchenka played on the keyboard of her sexual attraction in order to bring poor Dmitri into her nets. It is a typical cat-and-mouse game. Literature abounds with such examples, and one cannot help but feel sorry for the foolishness of the "strong sex" (as illustrated in Gogol's powerful novel *Taras Bulba*).

But it is not only women who can seduce men. Men can also seduce women. And even though generalization is risky, we are tempted to say that women are usually brought to their fall, not so much because of lust, but because of the promise of eternal love, or because they are told that their lover will kill himself if she does not yield to his wishes, or because of sheer vanity, or because they desperately want "to be wanted" and protected. How sweet it is to hear, "I have never seen a woman as beautiful as you are." "You are the only one who has ever touched my heart." The drama of Faust and Margarete comes to mind. It is so terribly tragic that when Margarete finds herself pregnant, abandoned, and in a desperate situation, she utters the words: "it was so good; it was so beautiful."[93] She nurtured the illusion that the "great" man who conquered her actually loved her and, when her eyes opened, she was threatened by despair.

Finally, more than men, women speak about their aches and pains. When sick, men may grumble but dislike making of their discomfort the topic of conversation. Usually women grieve more than men and worry about possible dangers before they become actual. If they yield to this tendency, their behavior can easily become irrational. Women are more likely than men to panic when they face a practical problem. The latter feel challenged and often enjoy tackling technological difficulties; they want to find solutions to problems. Men usually refuse to think about problems until they actually take place and *they can do something about them.* They shun talking about things which they cannot change or influence. On the other hand, women — more than men — grasp intuitively the meaning and value of suffering. Chesterton claims that men are more pleasure-seeking than women. A friend of my husband who, for many years, was chaplain for both monks and nuns, told him that the latter were much more willing to make sacrifices over and above what was strictly commanded by the rule.

In all this, no intelligent woman can find ground for offense. As a matter of fact, to be reminded of one's weakness is, from a supernatural point of view, a grace. How many mistakes could we all have avoided if we had reminded ourselves that without God's help we can do nothing? How many blunders do we make because we act impulsively and overlook our weaknesses and limitations? How many sins, faults, mistakes, and stupidities can be traced back to the fact that their perpetrator did not realize (or did not want to realize) how weak he was and did not ask for advice? Instead of being offended when reminded of their weakness, supernaturally motivated women are grateful. To be conscious of one's weakness and to trust in God's help is the way to authentic strength and victory. This has been etched admirably by Saint Paul when he wrote: "It is when I am weak that I am strong."[94] In the liturgy dedicated to Saint Agnes—a young maid who suffered martyrdom—the Church writes: "O God who chooses what is feeble in the world" (*"qui infirma mundi eligis..."*). A few days after the feast of Saint Agnes, the Church celebrates another young female saint: Dorothy, virgin and martyr. Dom Guéranger comments, "The religion of Christ alone can produce in timid women, like the saint of today, an energy which at times surpasses that of the most valiant martyrs among men. Thus does our Lord glorify His infinite power, by crushing Satan's head with what is by nature so weak."[95] Once again, the key to their victory over their innate "weakness" is the supernatural.

Pros

If faults occur because of woman's weakness, in so many cases, far from being a negative characteristic, the weak, the fragile, the breakable, the vulnerable, the sensitive refers to objects or persons who have something particularly fine about them, and which, for this reason, are more easily wounded or destroyed. A set of Sèvres porcelain is to be delicately handled, whereas a pot of iron can be rudely treated without harm. Even though Saint Peter does not elaborate, we can assume that this was one of the meanings he had in mind when he wrote of women's weakness (i.e., women should be honored because of their frailty). In Mediaeval Europe, it was the glory of the troubadours to protect women, and to challenge anyone who failed to respect them. To kill defenseless women and children in the course of hostilities was traditionally considered ignoble. Don Quixote's mission was to respect, honor, and defend the "weak," and particularly women.

Moreover, the very frailty of women can turn out to be their strength. Their weakness appeals to pity; it can touch men's hearts and appeal to what is best in them, namely their chivalrous instinct to help those weaker than themselves. As mentioned above, there is an unwritten law that was respected (at least officially) until modern warfare took over: In emergencies, women and children were saved first. They were the first to go into lifeboats; they were the first to receive medical help. In daily life, it is rare indeed that a man turns down a woman's cry for help. Men appreciate being called upon, being given a chance to show their manliness, to play the role of a mediaeval knight whose glory was to protect the weak and even to engage in daring deeds to dazzle and conquer the beautiful lady of his love.[96]

It is true indeed that women can shed "alligator tears," the silly tears of self-pity, of self-centeredness, tears that respond to imaginary offenses, to wounded vanity. (Some men too can fall into this weakness!) But the fact that some tears are silly and illegitimate should not blind us to the fact that tears can be expressions of what is best and noblest in man. When Augustine, conquered by grace, decided to respond to God's call to change his life, he was not ashamed to sob. "The floods burst from my eyes, an acceptable sacrifice to you."[97] Not only did he cry, but he made a point of informing us that his "defeat" found its expression in tears of repentance.

The Church in her motherly wisdom offers her children a prayer for every need; she has one special one for the gift of tears: *educ de cordis nostri duritia lacrymas compunctionis* (draw from our hardened heart tears of compunction). A deep conversion is usually "baptized" in tears.

Granted that women cry easily, the question is "why do they cry?" This whole question edges on whether tears are legitimate or illegitimate. We live in a world in which tears are called for daily. King David wrote, "My eyes shed tears, because men do not keep thy law."[98] One of the beatitudes is "Blessed are those that mourn." Woe to those who do not cry when God is blasphemed, where odious paintings are exhibited and praised as "works of art," when some priests say sacrilegious masses, when children are daily abused, when people are tortured, when millions are starving. Tears are the proper response to brutality, injustice, cruelty, blasphemy, hatred. Christ wept when He saw Jerusalem, and when He came to Lazarus's tomb. Saint Francis of Assisi shed tears because "love was too little loved." As Virgil put it: *"Sunt lacrimae rerum"* ("these are tearful things," that is, situations that call for tears).[99]

Christ promises that in heaven all tears will be dried, and Kierkegaard comments about the sad condition of those who have never shed a tear. We should cry over the daily offenses to God, cry over our sins, cry over the ingratitude of man. The most holy of all women, Mary, is called the *mater dolorosa* (sorrowful mother). Her immense sorrow has been admirably expressed by Giacopone da Todi, in his sublime poem dedicated to the sorrows of Christ's mother.[100] "Is there one who would not weep, whelm'd in miseries so deep Christ's dear mother behold." A woman's way to holiness is clearly to purify her God-given sensitivity and to direct it into the proper channels. She should fight against maudlin tears and pray for holy tears—tears of love, of gratitude, of contrition.

We have said that women are more attuned to their emotions than men, and that this can lead to serious faults. There are cases in which the heart is wrong (hypertrophy of the heart).[101] A woman's heart can degenerate into a virgin forest which calls for pruning. Nevertheless, there are situations when the heart is right and "reason" has become derailed, fallen into cheap rationalism characterized by the stubborn refusal to admit that many great truths transcend reason. Rationalism is allergic to "mysteries." Pascal must have had this in mind when he wrote, "The heart has its reasons that reason does not know of,"[102] and "The last proceeding of reason is to recognize that there is an infinity of things which are beyond it."[103] Finally, "There is nothing so conformable to reason as this disavowal of reason."[104]

Women, too, have a mission toward the other sex: the one of awakening and refining man's affectivity, often atrophied by abstractionism. They are definitely called upon to "humanize him." In his matchless, humorous way, Chesterton speaks about "feminine dignity against masculine rowdiness."[105] A man's heart can be a desert desperately in need of water. We all know men who are "thinking machines" and are dehumanized. The humorous and, at times, merciless Kierkegaard never missed a chance of making a thrust at his deadly enemy, Hegel. He hints at the fact that Hegel's "marriage must therefore have been as impersonal as his thought."[106] He clearly wishes us to feel sorry for Mrs. Hegel!

How beautiful is the complementariness of men and women according to the Divine Plan. It is not by accident that Saint Francis of Assisi was best understood by Saint Clare; Saint Francis of Sales by Saint Jeanne Françoise de Chantal; Saint Vincent of Paul by Louise de Marillac. In our own times, Marie Pila was co-foundress with Father Eugène Marie of Notre Dame de Vie in the Provence. Man is made for communion and the most perfect form of communion calls for persons who complement each other. This is why God said: "it is not good for man to be alone."

Female interests are centered on the human side of their lives: their family life, their relationships to those they love, their concern about their health, their welfare and, if they are Christians, the spiritual welfare of their children's souls; in other words, about human concerns. Most men speak about the stock market, politics, and sports; some speak about intellectual and artistic questions. Chesterton was right when he wrote, "Women speak to each other; men speak to the subject they are speaking about."[107]

· ∼ ·

A woman's mission is much aided by the very
beauty which, as we have seen, she can use for her
own downfall. A woman's loveliness (with all its
delicacy) can exercise such a charm upon her male
counterpart that her very frailty brings him to his
knees. This truth is poignantly highlighted in the
Old Testament when the lovely Queen Esther, in
order to save her people who were threatened by
the viciousness of the king's minister, daringly
broke the rule prohibiting anyone from coming to
King Ahasuerus without permission. Upon seeing
her entering into his apartment, "he (the king)
looked on her, blazing with anger." The queen sank
down. She grew faint, and the color drained from
her face, and she leaned her head against the maid
who accompanied her. "But God changed the
king's heart, inducing a milder spirit. He sprang
from his throne in alarm and took her in his arms
until she recovered, comforting her with soothing
words…'What is the matter, Esther?' He said, 'I
am your brother. Take heart; you will not die; our
order only applies to ordinary people. Come to me.'
And raising his golden scepter he laid it on her
neck, embraced her and said, 'speak to me.'"[108]
Thanks to God's help, her weakness conquered.
Her very frailty was the trump which made her victorious. She invited the king to a feast in the course

of which she begged him to save her life and the lives of her people. She disclosed to her husband the plans that his minister Haman had devised to exterminate the Jews. We all know the end of the story: The wicked Haman died on the very gallows he had set up for them.

Though different, a moving parallel—emphasizing beauty, frailty, and the power of tears all at once—is to be found in the life of Saint Scholastica, the sister of Saint Benedict, the Father of Western monasticism. Let us recall the touching episode of the last visit that Saint Benedict had with his holy sister. According to the rule, they could see each other only once a year. Their joy was to talk about God and sing His praise together. She begged her brother to prolong this holy colloquy, but he sternly refused: the rule ordered him to spend the night in his monastery. His gentle sister started praying, shielding with her hands the flood of tears streaming from her eyes. The sky which had been radiantly serene, suddenly became dark and threatening, and a fierce downpour accompanied by lightning and thunder forced Saint Benedict to remain for the night. This episode is related by Saint Gregory, and the Liturgy concludes this moving scene by stating, *"plus potuit, quia plus amavit"* ("having the stronger love, she had the stronger power").[109] This gentle virgin wept: but these tears were blessed tears, tears of tenderness, tears of love, tears that moved the heart of Christ—*fons ardens caritatis*—to order the heavens to produce a storm of such violence that Saint Benedict was forced to concede defeat. The strong one had to yield because God was on the side of the frail one.

God has indeed created women to be beautiful ("the sons of God saw that the daughters of men were fair…").[110] Their charm, lovableness, and beauty exercise a powerful attraction on the male sex, and it should be so. It is noteworthy that feminine loveliness contradicts the biological norm: Usually the male animal is more beautiful than the female one. The lion is more beautiful than the lioness; the rooster is more beautiful than the hen; the male duck has brilliant colors which are denied its female partner. This is one feature, among many, which points to the fact that sexuality in animals and human beings is radically different. For no one (except Schopenhauer) would deny that women are or can be beautiful. It is not by accident that they are called "the fair sex."

Innocent little girls can have a sweetness and charm that most fathers cannot resist. I know some who can be very stern toward their sons, but cannot bring themselves to deny the requests of their little girls who do not know as yet how lovely they are. With age (especially after puberty) most girls become conscious of the power they can exercise over men. Those whose hearts are noble or have been purified by grace will never use their charm to play with the strong sex, or worse to "seduce" it to gain their own subjective ends. They will put their gift at the service of the good and not at the service of evil. This was the case with Esther. She was not seeking any personal advantage. She wanted to save her people, and she accepted the risk of being sacrificed in order to achieve this noble end. She did not intend the death of Haman (even though he was, in fact, executed); she wanted to liberate her people.

We all know that there are women who, conscious of the power that the female sex has over men, do not hesitate to use it in order to achieve their own selfish ends. When a man commits fornication or adultery, we say "he went to his mistress." Clearly the word "mistress" indicates who is in command. The power that women can wield over men is great indeed. If they pursue their own selfish aims, women are Satan's slaves. If they put their charm at God's service, they are *God's great allies*. How often have I heard men say, "It is my wife who brought me back to God." "It is, above all, by means of woman that piety is first awakened and spreads its mysterious influence over society.... woman is one of the grand instruments of which Providence makes use to prepare the way for civilization...should she prove false to her high mission, society would perish."[111]

"In the whole evangelical history," says M. De Maistre, "women play a very remarkable part; and in all the celebrated conquests made by Christianity, either over individuals or over nations, there has always been some woman's influence."[112]

PART V

The Transfiguration of Weakness: The Incarnation

This mystery is so great that no human mind can exhaust it. Not only does it illumine the greatness of God's love for His creatures, not only does it give to matter a dignity which is a radical condemnation of gnosticism in all its forms, but it gives to woman an unheard-of dignity. Kierkegaard rightly remarked that a humble laborer would never imagine that a mighty emperor knew of his existence.[113] And let us imagine that the mighty emperor not only knew of his existence, but was willing to die in order to redeem him. This is something that could never have entered a man's head. *Christianity is true because it is above human invention.* Poets and writers have expressed man's longing to ascend higher. But no one, absolutely no one, either in the Eastern or in the Western world, has ever conceived of the thought that an infinitely perfect God, the second person of the Holy Trinity, would choose to assume man's imperfect nature, to be born of a woman (thereby giving to the female sex an unheard-of dignity), to know hunger, thirst, fatigue, suffering, and to experience the most brutal, the most terrible form of death out of love for sinful creatures. This can only be explained by "divine madness." Christ, the almighty and all-powerful one, *chose to become weak*, to teach men humility. For He shared all human traits except sin. His teaching aims at opening men's minds and hearts to the fact that their "strength" is mere illusion, "For without Me, you can do nothing." He told us that "unless we become like little children" we shall not enter into the kingdom of God. The child becomes the model we are invited to follow: his weakness, his helplessness, his total dependence upon others, his fragility. What a lesson for the proud Pharisees who relied heavily upon their learning and "perfection."

Saint Paul sheds further light upon this theme in his epistles. Both in Corinthians I and II he praises "weakness." He writes, "Has not God made foolish the wisdom of the world? The weakness of God is stronger than men."[114] And in his second epistle, the great apostle develops the same theme: "If I must boast, I will boast of the things that show my weakness."[115] After having hinted at the amazing graces that he has received, he adds: "...but on my own behalf, I will not boast except of my weaknesses."[116] In view of this praise of weakness, how can women be offended when they are called "the weaker sex?"

The same praise of "weakness" is to be found in the works of Saint Augustine. He tells us that his beloved friend Alypius, who had sworn never again to look at the cruel games of the Roman gladiators, relied too much upon his own strength, and once, when his friends dragged him into the games, he swore to himself that he would keep his eyes closed. But when the crowd suddenly started shouting from excitement, he could not help but open his eyes.[117] It was only when Alypius humbly acknowledged his weakness that he overcame this temptation. Saint Augustine himself, while desperately trying to live chastely, suffered repeated defeats. It was only when he realized that he could not achieve victory by his own strength and relied exclusively upon God's grace that he was freed from the shackles which had kept him prisoner for so long. True strength is knowing how weak one is, because this awareness is a clarion call that one needs help. God always listens to those who beg Him to come to their aid. What a sweet victory when the victor refuses to have laurels put on his own head and gives all the credit to his beloved, his Savior, his Holy Physician. Indeed, it is only when we acknowledge our weakness, as Saint Augustine came to do, that we become strong: "When I hear my former life brought forward, no matter with what intention it is done, I am not so ungrateful as to be afflicted thereat; for the more they show up my misery (weakness), the more I praise my physician."[118] Women definitely have an advantage over the strong sex because it is easier for them to acknowledge that they are weak and depend on divine help. This is why the Liturgy dubbed them "the pious sex."

This might be aptly called "the Christian revolution," a scandal for the Jews and a foolishness for the gentiles. It is the melody sung by one saint after another. It finds a particularly moving formulation and fulfillment in Saint Thérèse of Lisieux's "little way": To be unknown, to be hidden, to be regarded as insignificant and mediocre, to welcome one's "smallness," and misery. She rejoiced when she made a mistake, not because of the mistake, but because she was given a chance to taste, once again, her weakness and helplessness without God's grace. *The Story of a Soul* is a magnificent praise of weakness joyfully accepted and transformed by grace into supernatural victory. Let me repeat: It is sweet for someone who loves to give credit for victory to the beloved, a beloved who is all powerful, and often chooses "what is weak and helpless" to overcome the proud illusion that men are strong and do not need help. From a supernatural point of view there is nothing, absolutely nothing, which cannot be turned to God's glory. *Every defeat can become a vic-*

tory, every humiliation a precious jewel in one's crown, every suffering a glorious mark that makes the sufferer resemble his Savior. The alcoholic declaring publicly at an AA meeting that he is hooked on booze thereby changes his humiliating defeat into a magnificent victory.

The following passage in *The Story of a Soul* is revealing: "Ah! Poor women, how they are despised. And yet many more women than men love God. During Christ's passion, they showed more courage than the apostles for they braved the insults of the soldiers and dared to dry the adorable face of Jesus. For this reason, He allows women to be treated with contempt on earth, since He has chosen it for Himself. In heaven, He will show that His thoughts are not men's thoughts (Isaiah 55:8–9) for then the last will be the first."[119]

In Benedictine spirituality, the monks pray seven times a day: *"Deus in adjutorium meum intende; Domine, ad adjuvandum me festina"* ("God, come to my aid; hasten to help me"). Recognizing once again that we constantly need divine help and support not to fall into the nets that the wicked one keeps putting in front of us. Indeed, he is like a "roaring lion" seeking whom he can devour.[120]

When a person called by God enters religious life, he undergoes a period of trial called the novitiate. *One of its main purposes is to destroy the novice's natural self-assurance* and to replace it by an ever-greater realization of his weakness, of the fact that without God "he can do nothing." The master of novices will show him that his *natural virtues are unbaptized* and need to be purified. He will gently but firmly lead his charge to acquire supernatural virtues based on humility, that is, a total distrust of oneself and a total confidence in God's grace. The natural self-assurance of the novice is replaced by a holy "insecurity": in other words, a constant awareness of one's misery and a boundless confidence in Him who can raise children to Abraham out of stone.

PART VI

Women's Supernatural Mission

Against the background of what has been said, we can now perceive the beauty of femininity as coming out of God's loving hand, and the glorious mission assigned to it when fecundated by the supernatural. In an enlightening talk which Edith Stein (now known as Saint Edith Stein) delivered in Salzburg in 1930, she offered a masterful presentation of the differences which mark the male and the female nature. Women are more interested in persons than in things, she claims. And this is true indeed. Let us imagine the following scenario: A group of men and women are gathered behind a closed door. When the door is opened, they all enter a large room where only two things are to be found: a cradle with an infant in it on one side, and a brand new computer on the other. Women will flock to the cradle; men (after having given a brief glance at the baby) will opt for the masterpiece of technology and will start "playing" with it with passion. Women will rush to cuddle the baby and will radiate when the little one starts cooing. Obviously women are right, for a child is a marvel of God's creation that no technological accomplishment can match. Deep down, men must know that women have made the better choice, but it is hard for them to resist the fascination of technology.

Moreover, women place the concrete over the abstract, individuals over universals. Once again they are right. To make this claim does not denigrate the awesome world of abstraction, which certainly deserves our intellectual admiration. But it should be clear that the one concrete true God, the *"Deus vivens et videns"* of Saint Augustine, is metaphysically superior to the noble Platonic world of ideas. Great metaphysicians have understood that the ultimate reality cannot be an abstraction. The abstract, however great it might be, is metaphysically "thin" in that it lacks personhood. It is luminously clear that the one true God cannot be an "idea," a principle. He must be a person.

The female psyche is more responsive to the personal than to the impersonal. Women respond thus intuitively, without much deliberation, because they "feel" that persons rank infinitely higher than nonpersonal beings. What an abyss lies between an impersonal "deity" and the one personal God of the Old and New Testament, a God Who is a father, Who loves, Who instructs us, Who warns us, and when necessary, punishes us. Here again women score another metaphysical victory. Any sound metaphysics respects the hierarchy of being and places persons above things, living things above nonliving ones. The one true God is the God of life; Christ is the life of the soul, and women, who have the sublime mission of giving life, intuitively weave this principle into their daily lives. Eve was called "the mother of the living." There is a metaphysical bond between womanhood and life, and this is an honor indeed. This is why a woman, when she freely chooses to abort her child (without any pressure from boyfriend or parents) not only commits a grave sin but wounds her feminine nature to its very core. This is why it takes so long for such women to "recover" once their eyes have opened and they fully realize that they have betrayed their sacred mission. They are then threatened by self-hatred and tempted by suicide. They desperately need the loving help of a holy priest or a wise counselor to comfort them and assure them that God's mercy is infinitely greater than our sins, terrible as these may be. It is a mission desperately needed today, when millions of women have either chosen or allowed their children to be murdered—and in so doing, they have mortally wounded their souls.

Edith Stein further claims that women are more interested in wholes than in parts. Their minds do not dissect an object; they grasp it in totality. This is stated, again, not to denigrate the analytic power of men's minds, but to show that the female nature is structurally (i.e., without deliberation) geared to what is metaphysically higher. Because their minds and their hearts are closely related (their minds work best when animated by their hearts), their grasp of persons and objects does not fall into the traps which threaten specialists, who no longer see the forest because of the trees. Many great minds specialize so much in one facet of reality that they lose sight of the whole picture. Chesterton might have had this in mind when he wrote that "Cleverness shall be left for men and wisdom for women."[121] A similar thought has been expressed by John Bartlett: "Women are wiser than men because they know less but understand more."[122] For wisdom is not scholarship and the latter is often the refuge of people who have diplomas, who spend their lives bent on books but forget to live! A simple Italian peasant woman, say Mama Margarita—the saintly mother of Don Bosco—certainly possessed a remarkable wisdom as educator, a wisdom which is, alas, very often denied to "experts" in child psychology.

Another great gift that God has granted the female nature is the gift of receptivity. This is not to be confused with passivity as Aristotle does when he claims that the male is superior to the female because he is "active," whereas she is passive. Clearly passivity is inferior to activity, for one is only being "acted upon." But this is not true of receptivity which involves an alert, awakened, joyful readiness to be fecundated by another person or by a beautiful object. All created persons are essentially receptive because "there is nothing that we have not received."[123] Women feel at home in this receptivity and move in it with ease and grace. This is already inscribed in their biological nature: a wife giving herself to her husband accepts joyfully to be fecundated, to receive. Her receptivity is a self-giving.

But the marvel of childbirth is that even though she has only received a living seed—so microscopic that it is invisible to the human eye—after nine months she gives her spouse a human being, with an immortal soul made to God's image and likeness. The moment of conception takes place hours after the marital embrace, but when the sperm fecundates the female egg we can assume (even though it has never formally been taught by the Church) that at that very moment God creates the child's soul—a totally new soul which, being immaterial, cannot be produced by human beings. God therefore "touches" the female body in placing this new soul into the temple of her womb. This is another incredible privilege that the Creator grants to women. During pregnancy, she has the extraordinary privilege of carrying two souls in her body. If those unfortunate women who consider having an abortion were conscious of this, it is most unlikely that any of them would consent to the crime.

It is worth mentioning that while it is the husband who fecundates his wife, one says "she has given herself to him," implying that this receptivity is also a unique donation: To accept to receive is a very special gift. There are some unfortunate persons who would prefer to die than to receive, for the very thought of being indebted is repulsive to them. Kierkegaard writes about the demonic despair in which a man prefers the torments of hell to accepting help, "the humiliation of becoming nothing in the hands of the helper for whom all things are possible...."[124] To accept her state of creaturehood is easier for a woman than for a man, who is always tempted to be in command. How many men revolt at their metaphysical dependence; how many men resent being sick and weak and therefore forced to rely on the help of others?

Authentic creativity in creatures depends upon their degree of receptivity; to use Platonic language, he who produces without having opened himself to fecundation by God will produce "bastards." Much of what is called "modern art" falls into this category, because the temptation of many artists today is no longer to serve, but to "express" themselves. In this context, Gertrud von le Fort writes: "The artist who no longer gives God the honor, and instead proclaims only himself, must, by excluding the religious element from culture, practically eliminate also its womanly quality."[125]

In childbirth, this creative miracle that stems from womanly receptivity is, as we saw, exemplified in a unique way. It finds its climax in the words of the Blessed Virgin who only said "yes" to God's offer; she did not "do" anything, she simply said: "be it *done* to me according to Thy word." As soon as she uttered these holy words, she conceived the Savior of the world in the mystery of her blessed womb. She carried in the temple of her female organs the King of the Universe Whom the whole universe cannot contain. Important as the role of the father is, women collaborate in a very special way with God's creation of new human beings who are called upon to serve Him in this life and enjoy Him forever in heaven.

Receptivity is a religious category par excellence. The key to holiness is to let oneself be totally "reformed" by divine grace, to say to God, "do with me whatever you will." Mary said to the servants at the wedding in Cana, "Do whatever He tells you." That is the way to holiness. Because this characteristic is so crucial in religious life, it explains why the liturgy calls women "the pious sex." As long as women are faithful to their "religious" calling the world is safe. But the threat menacing us today is precisely the metaphysical revolt of feminists who have totally lost sight of their vocation *because they have become blind to the supernatural.*

At the turn of the century, the French academy offered a prize to the person who best answered the following question: "Why are there more men than women in jails?" The award was given to the person who wrote, "because there are more women than men in churches." One dreads to think of the possibility that "the pious sex" would let itself be convinced that prayer is only for the weak and the incompetent, meaningless for those aiming at greatness. Here is a truth worth meditating upon: Women are more geared to piety because they have a keener awareness of their weakness. This is their true strength.[126]

PART VII

Women and Feelings

Feelings are often denigrated in homilies and in spiritual direction. Women are told that spiritual life is based not on emotions, but on faith, will, and rational thought. If by feelings we mean the flow of irrational emotions that, like flies, keep swarming around us, this advice should be taken very seriously. No doubt feelings can be dangerous and misleading. But as my late husband has convincingly shown in his book *The Heart,* the word "feeling" is equivocal.[127] Failure to clarify such ambiguities will necessarily lead to a disparaging of feelings. Aristotle claimed that whereas intelligence and free will are human prerogatives, feelings are experiences that man shares with animals. In claiming that feelings are shared by men and animals, Aristotle must have been thinking of localized physical sensations (such as pain and pleasure), which indeed man shares with animals. Both men and animals can feel cold, hunger, thirst, fatigue; all of these experiences are related to the body and are located in the body. They are "voices of the body."[128] *A partial truth is not an error.* But, when this partial truth is extended to include all types of feelings, it definitely becomes an error and a serious one. The above-mentioned experiences share one common feature: they are *unintentional,* which—in the vocabulary of Husserl—means that no knowledge of their cause is necessary in order for these "feelings" to be experienced. They are definitely nonspiritual, and man shares them with animals.[129]

Feelings can refer secondarily to experiences which are very different from this first type: We are thinking of "psychic feelings" such as moods, depression (caused by a physical condition), the jolliness which most people experience when drinking alcoholic beverages, and so on. These feelings have no bodily location—as the first clearly do—but they share with the first their lack of intentionality. One need not know their cause in order to experience them.[130]

Radically different are "spiritual feelings," which have neither a bodily location nor lack intentionality. They cannot possibly arise in man's soul unless he has an awareness of what *motivates* these feelings. One cannot love without knowing what or whom one loves, without realizing that this love is a response to a lovable object; one cannot hate without an awareness that this feeling arose as a response to something or somebody hateful. One cannot be grateful without knowing what we are grateful for and to whom we are indebted. Chesterton does remark, however, that at one point in his early life, he found himself in the ludicrous situation of feeling grateful "...though I hardly knew to whom."[131]

These feelings share with intelligence and will the feature of intentionality; that is why they fully deserve to be called "spiritual." Our responses to the objects or persons motivating our feeling can be appropriate or not. Because of original sin, man is, alas, capable of giving wrong and distorted responses. One can hate what is lovable; one can rejoice over evil deeds; one can be saddened by the happiness of other persons, and be elated by their unhappiness (*schadenfreude*). In such cases, our illegitimate response creates a cacophony, a false note in the symphony of the universe. *It should not be.*

But, with God's grace, man is capable of transcending his narrow subjectivism, his tendency to look at events exclusively from the point of view of his interest, and give what my late husband called "a value response," that is, to love what deserves to be loved, to love more what is higher, to love less what is lower.[132] Centuries ago, Plato wrote that one of the aims of education is to teach the child "...to hate what should be hated and to love what should be loved."[133] By hearkening to this message, man joins his humble voice to the symphony of the universe, proclaiming God's greatness, beauty, and truth.

It is noteworthy that these spiritual responses not only share the features that intellect and will possess, (e.g., one cannot love without knowing the object of one's love), but *surpass them in richness and plenitude.* In spiritual response, man's intellect is fully activated. The role of the will is also crucial, for our spiritual affective responses must be "sanctioned" by our will (in my husband's terminology); this sanctioning makes them truly to become ours. All feelings which have not been "sealed" by our will, are likely to wither and die. Like the statues of Daedalus, they must be "nailed" to gain their full validity.[134] What a difference exists between a person feeling compassion and one strengthened by a will to be compassionate and, therefore, anxious to act compassionately when actions are called for. The folly of claiming that one is compassionate and yet refusing to help has been ironically expressed in a play of Nestroy, an Austrian playwright: A rich man witnessing the abject misery of a beggar orders his servants to "throw this beggar down the steps; his misery breaks my heart." What a difference there is between a feeling of contrition and the will to go to confession and ask for forgiveness.

Feelings are further viewed as "inferior" because they cannot be commanded. But this argument is unconvincing: Grace cannot be commanded by the will either, not because it is "inferior" but because it is "superior." It is an unmerited gift. Those who have experienced moments of radiant spiritual joy and profound peace know that these feelings are "gifts" for which we should be grateful, and which God can take away from us when He so wishes. Saint Teresa of Avila writes emphatically that spiritual joys should not be "sought" and pursued. When received, they call for gratitude. But our heart should not rest in them and lose its peace when they are taken away.

The crucial role played, however, by the will in spiritual feelings is strikingly expressed in both the ceremony of marriage and the taking of religious vows: The bride, the bridegroom, or the novice makes a solemn declaration that gives to their love of each other or of God its full validity. The fiancés love each other; the postulant loves God. Now they ardently want to formalize this feeling, and give it its full weight and plenitude by declaring solemnly that even though their feeling of love for each other or for God may wane (due to the frailty of human nature, due to physiological conditions, due to periods of trial), they know that these feelings (which may be hidden from them in the mystery of their souls) are still fully (superactually) present and valid, because they are ratified by their wills. This remains fully true even though the joy of experiencing love has momentarily been taken away from them. Love will continue to manifest itself in acts of kindness, faithfulness, and prayer in moments of total aridity. These are periods of trial during which one can prove one's faithfulness (*fides* means both "belief" and "faithfulness"). How many saints have gone through a period of intense dryness during which they no longer "felt" that they loved God, but persevered at His service with heroic courage. Very often, this cross was taken from them shortly before death. Saint John of the Cross has described more eloquently than anyone else "the dark night of the soul." The crucial point is that "love" is still there, but no longer experienced, no longer a source of delight. The saint then walks in the darkness of faith. But it is a sign of man's greatness how freely he can deny himself the freedom to change his mind: This is the very essence of vows.

Therefore the traditional suspicion that many religiously minded people have had toward feelings is unwarranted. True, our feelings must be purified, but this is equally true of our intellect and of our will. Kierkegaard wrote that the sins of the intellect are often worse that the sins of passions (derailed affectivity): "Oh! The sins of passions and of the heart, how much nearer to salvation than the sins of reason."[135] In his powerful novel *Oblomov*, Goncharov puts the following words in the mouth of his heroine: "...it is a bad habit with men to be ashamed of their heart. That is false pride. They had better be sometimes ashamed of their intellect—it goes astray more often."[136] The point is that it is our heart which is vulnerable and, therefore, *makes us realize our weakness*, which is distasteful to masculine pride. It was the heart of Christ that was pierced by the soldier's spear. Because our spiritual feelings come from our heart, and because man's heart must be transformed from a heart of stone into a heart of flesh, it is clear that purification of spiritual feeling is crucial in the process of man's sanctification.[137]

The heart (the tabernacle of affectivity) symbolizes the whole person. When one falls in love, one says to the beloved, "I give you my heart." It would be strange indeed if one said "I give you my intellect, or my will, or my memory." It is written in the Bible: "Give me your heart."[138] But it is also true that the human heart can incarnate wickedness and corruption.[139] It therefore symbolizes the best and the worst in man. Man's daily prayer should be "make my heart like unto yours." In the saints and in the wise, intellect, will, and heart are fully purified.

The nobility of right feelings and their importance in spiritual life is powerfully illustrated in the autobiographies of both Saint Teresa of Avila and Saint Thérèse of Lisieux. How often they use the word "feeling," yet, hopefully, no one would dare accuse them of subjectivism and illusionism. When asked by her confessor how she knew that it was Christ that was present to her, the great Spanish

mystic answered that she "felt it" (*"lo sentia"*).[140]
She was right, for He truly was present to her. But
she also was fully aware, from having to deal with
many nuns, that feelings can be the fruits of self-
centeredness, sentimentality, emotionalism, or
oversusceptibility, so she waged a relentless war
against these crippling dangers. She knew that we
can "feel" offended or deeply hurt, or wounded because we have been justly criticized.[141]

The liturgy of the Holy Church gives testimony to
the role of the heart in religious life; she has blessed
us with a litany to the Sacred Heart of Jesus. There
is no litany dedicated to the divine intellect or the
divine will. When Christ in agony spoke the heartbreaking words—"I am thirsty"—the Holy One
was thirsting for our love. The heart is where love
resides. The heart needs to be vindicated and this
can best be achieved by distinguishing between
valid and invalid feelings, legitimate and illegitimate
feelings, "baptized feelings and unbaptized ones."
Failing to "discriminate" between them inevitably
leads to a denigration of this rich field of human
experiences, and was bound *to have a negative effect
on women* who, traditionally, have been called "the
heart of the family."

The greatest and deepest religious and human experiences are related to the heart. It is our heart that

makes us vulnerable. The heart of the Savior was "bruised by our sins."[142] It is the heart that loves, that is merciful, that has compassion, that feels contrition, that cries over sins, that is wounded by wickedness. Saint Francis' heart was bleeding "because love was so little loved." It is the heart that suffers *with* the beloved and would be happy to suffer *for* the beloved. Christ tells us that "He is meek and humble of heart."

Spiritual guidance aims at purifying man's intellect and leading it to an ever-greater and deeper knowledge of truth; it aims at strengthening the will. But wise spiritual guidance should show great concern not only for the elimination of illegitimate feelings, but also for the blossoming of noble, sublime, and generous feelings which flower in a pure heart. That holiness carries with it a transformation of the heart is shown best by the tenderness that great male saints exude. Let us think of Saint Bernard and his homily upon the death of his beloved brother, Gerard: "Cruel death! By taking away one, thou has killed two at once; for the life which is left to me is heavier than death."[143] Saint Francis of Sales also comes to mind: his innumerable letters express a sweetness admirably combined with holy manliness. These saints, masterpieces of God's grace, combine all great male virtues with female gentleness. Great female saints, while keeping the perfume of female gentleness, can show a strength and courage that sociology usually reserves to the male sex. It is typical of the supernatural that such apparently contradictory features can be harmoniously united.

Some may claim that the metaphysical inferiority of feelings is clearly proven by the fact that the body is involved with them (for example, our heart beats faster when we experience a great joy or fear). To deny that physical manifestations of profound spiritual experiences can validly and meaningfully be expressed in the human body is a prejudice that should be eradicated from a Christian mind. From the beginning, Christianity has waged war on any form of gnosticism—this ever-recurring error of despising the flesh, born of pride. For the Word itself became flesh. Since the greatest event in history took place, it is clear that we should not despise physical manifestations of deep psychic and spiritual experiences. This truth is also expressed in the Canticle of Canticles: *"stipate me malis, quia amore langueo"* ("refresh me with apples, for I am sick with love").[144] Man is a union of body and soul; just as the body will partake of man's beatitude or of his damnation, it is proper and classical that in the course of this earthly life, the body should mirror the experiences of the soul. Far from being an indication of inferiority, the connection between body and emotion sheds light on the deep link existing between man's body and his soul. The most powerful manifestation of the union between soul and body is to be found in the phenomenon of stigmata. One certainly can reach sainthood without duplication of the wounds of our Savior. But that there are cases, fully validated, in which man's body partakes of the tortures that Christ suffered when crucified, is a powerful expression of both the union of body and soul, and of the closeness which exists between a creature burning with love for its creator, and gratefully partaking in the immensity of His pains.

Saint Benedict has understood this union so deeply that, in his Rule, he keeps stressing the importance in religious life of a reverent bodily posture. It does make a difference whether man kneels or stands, whether one bows or not, whether one sits straight or yields to "the law of gravity." One of the regrettable things which have taken place in the wake of Vatican II is that all these so-called "exterior" manifestations of piety which speak to the senses of the body have been abolished. Statues have been removed from our Churches; the violet cloths that used to cover statues from Passion Sunday onward are no longer used. So many exterior reminders that we are here on this earth to serve God have been eliminated, with all the deplorable consequences that we now know. In my home country, what used to be Catholic Belgium, one could not take a walk in the beautiful forest surrounding the capital, or in the countryside, without seeing small little chapels dedicated to Christ, His Holy Mother, or some saint. It was a constant reminder that faith should animate all our actions. The devil is a master psychologist and knows exactly how much we depend upon visual perceptions to buttress our faith. Destroying the physical signs of faith that move our affective reception certainly was not ordered by the texts of Vatican II. Who is the culprit?

The great defense of the body and the nobility of its relation to feeling is the profound fact of the Resurrection. How deeply Christian is the dogma of the resurrection of the body: To be human is to be a person incarnated in a body. It is therefore proper and just that this companion of our earthly life should partake in the glory or ignominy of our eternal fate. Man's soul is immortal and survives the destruction of his body; but the fullness of human nature calls for the resurrection of the flesh. The soul can exist without the body, but is *widowed when the body dies;* it then longs for the reunion with its companion.

The conclusion we can draw from this brief survey of feelings is that it is unwarranted to regard women as inferior because feelings play a central role in their lives. If the feelings vibrating in their hearts are noble, appropriate, good, legitimate, sanctioned, and pleasing to God, then they are precious jewels in God's sight.

PART VIII

The Mystery of the Female Body

Saint Bonaventure writes that the world is like a book heralding the greatness of the Creator, but we must learn to read its message. He who has mastered this art through grace will discover that the contemplation of creation provides the soul with rich spiritual food. He whose eyes are opened will be able to decipher the divine message issuing from inanimate nature, plants, animals, clouds, the sky. They all sing the praise of the great King. Natural beauty speaks eloquently about the Beauty of the Creator that it modestly reflects. They are God's footprints (*vestigia*), Saint Bonaventure tells us.[145] Once this truth is grasped, Saint Paul's exhortation that we should be praying at all times becomes not only understandable, but easy to follow.[146] For everything in creation speaks of God, provided we are willing to open our eyes and ears to it. The same thought is expressed in Saint Francis of Sales. This gentle saint stresses repeatedly that the cosmos is rich in analogies elevating our minds and souls from the material to the spiritual, from the created to the Creator.[147]

A contemplation of the female body can yield rich insights into the mission of women. The first thing that comes to mind is that in her body the intimate organs are not visible. They are all "hidden" within her. In this, she differs clearly from her male counterpart. This fact is rich in symbolism: What is hidden usually refers to something mysterious, something that should be protected from indiscreet looks. The very structure of her body symbolizes a garden that should be carefully guarded, for the keys of this garden belong to God. It is His property in a special sense and is to be kept untouched until He allows the bride-to-be to give the keys to her husband-to-be of what is called, in the Canticle of Canticles, a *"hortus conclusus"* ("a closed garden").[148] How beautiful when, on the night of her wedding, the young bride can say to the bridegroom: "I have kept this garden unsullied for you; now that God has received our pledge to live our married life in His sight (*in conspectu Dei*), I am granted the permission to give you the keys to this garden, and I trust that you will approach it with fear and trembling." How very sad when this garden has already been trampled upon by impure feet and ravaged by lust. The bridegroom should be reminded that God's permission is required in order for him to penetrate into this sacred enclosure, and that he should do so with both reverence and gratitude.

The mysterious character of this garden is an emblem and a repetition, a *figura*, of the greatest event that has taken place in history: The Incarnation — God becoming man, hidden for nine months in the womb of the most perfect of all creatures — the Virgin Mary. That this event was wrapped in a deafening silence (Saint Joseph was not even informed) is profoundly meaningful. The world was forever changed, and no one knew about it except a humble Virgin. Secular events take place with a bang; God's mysteries are secret and hidden. This is why it was proper that this overwhelming event was buried in holy silence.

Not only are the female organs "hidden," they are also *veiled*. A veil symbolizes both mystery and sacredness. When Moses came down from Mount Sinai where he had been permitted to hear God's voice, he veiled his face as an appropriate response to his overwhelming privilege. In Catholic churches, the tabernacle is veiled when the divine host is present. This "veil" is so essential to femininity that Saint Augustine wrote that even when a female child is the fruit of rape, fornication, or adultery, her little body is not denied this mysterious covering.[149] The veil of virginity is a very special female privilege.

In view of the extraordinary dignity that virginity has acquired in Christian life, the biological make-up of women indicates that their reproductive organs are stamped by sacredness and belong to God in a special sense. Hence, woman's mission is to be the guardian of purity. In view of this insight, it becomes understandable that, traditionally, a woman who has sinned against the Sixth Commandment is more severely frowned upon than her male counterpart. In and by itself, this may strike one as a typical case of injustice: For in front of God, the sin of fornication or adultery is equally severe whether perpetrated by a man or by a woman. But when we realize that the intimate sphere is especially confided to women—that they should be the guardians of the virtue of purity—the severity of social censure on fallen women becomes more understandable. *When a particular mission is confided to some persons, and these persons fail to respond to its demands, it creates a greater metaphysical disharmony than when the same failure is to be found in someone who has not received this special calling.* By betraying this calling, they stain themselves in a special way. Even though grave injustices have been committed in this domain (how many women have been mercilessly ostracized from society because they have fallen, when men are often excused with the words, "they were sowing their wild oats"), this "injustice" is rooted in a tacit acknowledgment that women have received a special mission. Deep down, society understands that women's purity is a linchpin of any Christian society, nay, of any civilized society. When she betrays her mission, not only is God offended but in wounding herself spiritually she wounds the Church and society at large.

The union of body and soul is, in some way, particularly close in a woman's body. She is "incarnated" in her body in a special way. This is why, when she gives herself, she gives herself completely; when she stains herself, the stain is particularly damaging. But Catholicism, rich in mercy and in hope, teaches us that God can make all things new. Though "the rich worth of your virginity"[150] cannot be regained when lost, God's mercy, in response to tears of contrition, can nevertheless elevate the sinner and make her to become a great saint. Saint Mary Magdalene comes to my mind. The same is true of Saint Marguerite of Cortona.

On the other hand, those who have been protected by God's grace should humbly thank Him. They should say in their heart: "Not to us, O Lord, not to us, but to Thy name give glory."[151] Woe to the virgin whose purity is stained by pride, who gloats over her virginity, who feels "precious" and superior because "she is untouched," and harbors the erroneous belief that her "virtue" is due to her own merit. The words of Christ then come to mind: "…prostitutes will precede you in heaven."[152]

• ∼ •

Husband and wife are called upon to collaborate with God in the creation of another human being. But they must remember that being creatures they can only "procreate," they cannot create. Unless the husband's body has living seeds, unless the wife's body has eggs, the process of fertilization cannot take place. Some preexisting matter is not only necessary, it is essential in order for procreation to be realized. God alone can create the soul, it cannot originate from either parent. The soul is not made of some pre-existing matter. It is a totally new creation. Human beings cannot produce something out of nothing.

The special role granted to women in procreation, as mentioned before, is highlighted by the fact that as soon as she has conceived (and conception takes place hours after the marital embrace), God creates the soul of the new child *in her body*. This implies a direct "contact" between Him and the mother-to-be, a contact in which the father plays no role whatever. This contact gives to the female body a note of sacredness, for any closeness between God and one of His creatures is stamped by His Holy Seal. This divine "touch" is once again a special female privilege that every pregnant woman should gratefully acknowledge.

If sex education in our schools refrained from speaking about moral perversions and various methods of artificial birth control and instead taught these sublime Catholic truths, chastity would, once again, become for young people the luminous beacon that it had been for centuries when Catholic life was vibrant.

Childbirth is also an event basked in sacredness. Granted that the agonizing pains that many women endure are a dire consequence of original sin, the beauty of Catholic teaching makes it clear that her womanly travails and cries of agony, which precede the coming into the world of another human person, have a deeply symbolic meaning. Just as Christ has suffered the agonizing pains of the crucifixion in order to reopen for us the gates of heaven, so the woman has received the costly privilege of suffering so that another child made to God's image and likeness can enter into the world. In a similar context, Chesterton writes, "No one staring at that frightful female privilege, can quite believe in the equality of the sexes...."[153] During pregnancy, the mother-to-be actually carries two souls within herself: her own and the one of her baby. Chesterton must have had something similar in mind when he wrote, "Nothing can ever overcome that one enormous sex superiority, that even the male child is born closer to his mother than to his father."[154]

Our great concern throughout this book has been to eliminate the deeply rooted prejudice which foolishly asserts that the whole of Judeo-Christian tradition—and very particularly the Catholic Church—has discriminated against women. But the news media have been so efficient at propagating this new "gospel" that many nuns left their convents and joined the unhappy army of women whose vocation is to fight "sexism"—a newly discovered capital sin—which, in their eyes, is so grave that other offenses against God seem to pale by comparison. Such tragic aberrations are possible only in the souls whose sense of the supernatural has been warped, nay, destroyed.

THE MYSTERY OF FEMININITY

The woman is more mysterious than her male companion. On the artistic level, this is strikingly expressed in one of the greatest of all paintings, the *Mona Lisa* of Leonardo da Vinci. One can look at this masterpiece for hours; the more one looks at it, the more one feels the mystery that this female presence radiates. It is inconceivable that a male portrait could visibly express such an unfathomable depth. For this reason men often complain "that they cannot understand the female psyche." Being more "linear," more guided by rational considerations, less subtle, men must learn to "transcend" themselves in order to enter into a deep communion with their female counterpart. Women, too, will have to achieve a similar act of transcendence to understand man's psyche, but it is probably less difficult for them to do so than for men to understand women. She is, by nature, more receptive, more tuned to others. It is easier for her to feel empathy, to feel herself into others.

It is therefore appropriate to speak of the "mystery of femininity." This mystery is symbolized, as we saw, by the veil, which might be one of the reasons why Saint Paul recommended that women's heads should be covered in church. It is regrettable that this deeply meaningful custom which — far from demeaning women, as the feminists repeat *ad nauseam,* was a way of honoring them — has been abandoned after Vatican II, even though it was in no way demanded by the Council.

We have pointed out that the reproductive organs of the woman are hidden in her body; they are not "exterior," they are not visible. For these various reasons, it is justified to say that the "second sex" is wrapped in mystery; when women betray the mystery confided to them they hurt not only themselves, but society at large, and very especially the Church. The fearful sexual decadence that we have witnessed in the course of the last forty years can be traced back, at least in part, to the fashion world's systematic attempt to eradicate in girls the "holy bashfulness" which is the proper response that women should give to what is personal, intimate, and calls for veiling. To dress modestly is the appropriate response that women should give to their "mystery." *Noblesse oblige.* The fashions of the day are all geared toward destroying women's sensitivity for the dignity of their sex. Deep sadness is called for when one watches Western girls running around practically naked and then compare them with how the Hindu or Moslem women are clothed with modesty, grace, and dignity. No doubt, a mastermind has initiated these decadent fashions which aim at destroying female modesty.[155] The state of our contemporary society sheds light on the fact that when women "no longer know how to blush," it is a portent that this society is on the verge of moral collapse. Women carry a heavy share of guilt because they betray their human and moral mission. When women are pure, men will respect, nay, venerate them; they will also hear the call challenging them to chastity.

Education in modesty should begin at the earliest age. Little girls should be gently trained to respect their bodies. Saint Benedict understood deeply the effects that our body language, our bodily postures have on our souls. This includes one's way of dressing; one's way of sitting; not crossing one's legs in a manner which can be offensive, not wearing shorts which, although acceptable for the male sex, are likely to undermine the female respect for the mystery of her body.

It is noteworthy that whereas there are special masses for apostles, popes, bishops, confessors, abbots, and martyrs, for women there are only two categories: virgin and nonvirgin; martyrs and nonmartyrs. The Holy Bride of Christ dedicates a special liturgy for virgins. No such privilege exists for celibate priests. In so doing, the Church acknowledges the special dignity God has chosen to give to women. This seems to indicate that virginity differs from celibacy. Whereas *both* celibacy and virginity symbolize a total self-donation to God, virginity has an additional virtue: the consecration of an organ (namely the female womb) which, through God's infinite mercy, has sheltered the God-man for nine months. May we suggest that the fact that the female organs are hidden by a veil was a presaging that, in God's plans, a female womb was to hide the King of Glory, "Him that the whole universe cannot contain?"

If little girls were made aware of the great mystery confided to them, their purity would be guaranteed. The very reverence which they would have toward their own bodies would inevitably be perceived by the other sex. Men are talented at reading women's body language, and they are not likely to risk being humiliated when a refusal is certain. Perceiving women's modesty, they would take their cue and, in return, approach the female sex with reverence, instead of with today's brutal irreverence which unleashes lust and impurity.

• ∽ •

The secularistic gospel teaches us that sex is an instinct which in no way differs from other instincts such as hunger or thirst.[156] The theory prevalent today is that just as the latter instincts cry for fulfillment, the sexual "drive" has its own rights, and man should listen to its needs and respond to its message. Young people are told that sex is "healthy" and that to repress it can lead to all sorts of psychological disturbances, complexes, and so on. This secularistic gospel explains why, in the wake of Vatican II, many priests and nuns have broken their vows and married. Some of them literally panicked upon discovering that, being virgins, they were "psychologically" crippled. They naively believed that they had finally found the key to all their problems.

In fact, *it is not true that sex is an instinct like hunger and thirst.* Not only is sex always deep and serious (which cannot be said of other instincts), it is definitely meant to be at the service of the deepest human aspiration: love. It is love alone that gives sex its true meaning, which will forever remain hidden to the person who only perceives its biological aspect. That sex differs radically from other instincts should be clear from the fact that another person is involved. Food is inanimate and so is drink. But in sex man has a partner and this partner, being a person made to God's image and like-ness, must be approached with reverence. How many persons have been deeply wounded—maybe for life—because they have been played with! We use food as a means to satisfy our hunger, we drink water to quench our thirst, conscious of the fact that these inanimate objects are at our service; they are there "for us." Water is not "loved" for itself; it is a means to satisfy a need. But another human being, as Kant has clearly expressed, should never be used as a means.[157] Because of his dignity as a person, one's partner should be approached with reverence. He is not a tool; he is not a plaything which happens to give pleasure. For this reason alone, we can already understand the seriousness of the sexual sphere.

Moreover, because sex is related to something not only deep but intimate, it implies a self-revelation; as it is said in Genesis, "Adam knew Eve." This is a succinct but eloquent way of saying that, in the mu-tual donation of the spouses, they "reveal" in a way which is matchless. This self-revelation can only take place with God's express permission, for we belong to Him. At the same time, it is a self-donation which by its very nature calls for a total commitment to an-other person. One cannot give oneself to many per-sons simultaneously. One cannot "reveal" oneself to more than one person: the person with whom we are bound in the holy sacrament of matrimony.

Because of its sacredness, because it is deep, because the sexual sphere belongs to God in a special way, its abuse is always grave. To view the sexual sphere as "fun" is a desecration, and its abuse (when all conditions for sin are fulfilled: full consciousness and full willingness) constitutes a mortal sin that radically separates us from God. That desecration becomes still clearer when we recall that this sphere is linked to procreation—this mysterious collaboration between the spouses and God in the creating of another human being. To sever love from its fruitfulness is to sow the seed that will ultimately destroy it. It is not by accident that marriages which practice artificial birth control are those that break up most frequently.

People cannot live without a minimum of food and drink. True, some mystics have survived on the Holy Eucharist, but they were fed in a miraculous fashion. But it is a lie to claim that human beings become crippled if they have no sexual life. Innumerable saints of both sexes have led celibate lives or taken and kept a vow of virginity, but they all had radiant, fulfilled personalities, and often lived to a long, ripe age. Let us imagine how ludicrous it would be if all of a sudden a young person who seemed to enjoy a blooming health dropped dead; according to the laws of certain states, an autopsy must be performed on the corpse. How ridiculous it would be if, after hours of careful dissection of the dead person, the doctor would declare virginity to be the cause of her demise! Everyone knows that this does not make sense. But we all know people who die young because they have abused sex and caught diseases that unforgiving nature has linked to these aberrations.

We have mentioned several times that every sin brings with it its own punishment. Apart from the possibility of serious infections, lewd people will never taste the true beauty of a sexual union based on mutual love and lived in reverence. They certainly have tasted the poisonous violence of passion and an intensity of pleasure which, as Plato wrote centuries ago, nails the soul to the body.[158] But the sweetness of a mutual self-donation, accomplished in trembling reverence, will never be theirs.[159] Esau sold his birthright for a mess of pottage. Such unfortunate individuals place piggishness above love. Just as Freud devoted his life to the sexual sphere and never understood its deeper meaning, so the people whose god is sex will never experience its true meaning and beauty. Like Alberich in Wagner's ring-cycle, they will experience lust, but their punishment is that they will never taste the sweetness of true love.

MATERNITY

Whereas few men are called upon to become priests, all women, without exception, are called upon to be mothers. The saintly Cardinal Mindzenty has written a book about motherhood which—thanks to the inspiration and example given him by his holy mother—contains the most sublime reflections ever made about this topic. Indeed, "maternity is God's tenderness."[160] Maternity is the great female charism which corresponds to the charism of priesthood granted to some men. God has decided that these two charisms are not compatible.

In her book *The Eternal Woman*, Gertrud von le Fort writes: "To be a mother, to feel maternally, means to turn especially to the helpless, to incline lovingly and helpfully to every small and weak thing upon the earth."[161] The diabolical work that has taken place since the legalization of abortion is that it has destroyed, in those tragic women who have allowed their child to be murdered, their sense for the sacredness of maternity. Abortion not only murders the innocent; it spiritually murders women. Those who devote their loving attention to these victims of our decadent society know that the wound created in their souls is so deep that only God's grace can heal it. The very soul of the woman is meant to be maternal. Once this sublime calling has been trampled upon, such women become "unsexed;" they are "sick unto death." Maternity is a sublime calling, and even though man's ungrateful heart often forgets his mother's sufferings to bring him into the world and her endless devotion in order to bring him up, it is well-known that when a man faces death on the battlefield, his last words, his last thoughts are often directed to his mother. Dying soldiers scream, "Mother."[162]

PART IX

Mary and the Female Sex

The privilege of being a woman is particularly highlighted by the fact that Mary—the most perfect creature—was a woman. Every female child is, like the Holy Virgin, born with a mysterious veil hiding her feminine organs. Every woman has a womb; and this is a privilege because it was in a female womb that the Savior of the world was hidden. Every woman has breasts and every woman should meditate upon the fact that the King of the Universe was breastfed by the holiest of creatures. Every mother breastfeeding her child is doing exactly what took place in Bethlehem, Egypt, and Nazareth centuries ago. Because her female nature creates a deep bond between woman and the Holy Virgin, woman are called upon to imitate Mary's virtues: first and foremost, her radiant humility. Saint Augustine tells us that he found some admirable virtues among pagans (let us think of Socrates), but that never, absolutely never, did he find a pagan who possessed the virtue of humility.[163] The reason is that this virtue is possible only on the supernatural plane; it is therefore not accessible to those whose outlook is limited to natural ethics. The humble person dreads to be called humble, and actually suffers when someone praises him for possessing this elusive virtue. The proud person, on the contrary, loves to hear his "humility" commended and basks in this praise. As long as we compare ourselves to other human creatures—be it for physical, intellectual, or spiritual characteristics—we shall always find someone who is "worse" off than we are. We can easily console ourselves for our lack of talents by pointing to someone who is more deprived than we are. We all know persons who are ugly and yet who enjoy pointing to the still greater ugliness of someone whose "dowry" is more "anemic" than theirs.

But humility refrains from making purely human comparisons. This virtue teaches us to place ourselves naked in front of our Creator, the infinitely perfect and Holy One. Such a confrontation must bring us to our knees and force us to acknowledge that we are "nothing but dust and ashes" as Abraham said when he begged God to spare Sodom and Gomorrah. It is inconceivable that someone should stand in front of the one true God and persist in the illusion that he is "something." All the gifts we possess come from God; by ourselves we are *nothing,* and would fall back into nothingness if God's hand did not sustain us in existence through the *concursus divinus* (divine concurrence). This confrontation between God and man could be crushing and lead us to metaphysical despair (let us recall the cry of Saint Peter: "Depart from me, O Lord, for I am a sinful man").[164] But the recognition of our nothingness should go hand in hand with an awareness that God, the infinitely good and merciful God, loves his creatures, these poor beggars that He has knighted by making them to His image and likeness. The moment that man perceives both his misery and his greatness, the consciousness that he is loved brings him such overwhelming joy that, appropriately, he prefers to be nothing because the one who loves him and whom he has learned to love is everything.[165] A loving spouse rejoices in acknowledging the superiority of her spouse. What a joy to contemplate the perfections of the one we love. What a joy it is to sing a hymn of gratitude because this beautiful being deigns to love us. All the saints have found their delight in declaring their nothingness and their trust that "He can make great things in us."

This is the first great lesson that Mary teaches us, for her response to God's unfathomable gift is the *Magnificat*. Upon receiving the message that God had chosen her as the tabernacle in which His Divine Son would be incarnated, she expresses surprise. The favor offered her was something she felt so unworthy of. Moreover, she was a virgin: How can a virgin become a mother? But upon receiving the assurance that the Holy Spirit would cover her, she humbly declares herself to be the handmaid of the Lord, and actualizes the feminine charism of receptivity by saying: "be it *done* to me according to Thy Word." Knowing that this holy pregnancy will cause concern to Saint Joseph, who does not know the immense gift that his fiancée has received, she puts all her trust in God, knowing that He will protect the honor of His chosen one. Her faith is boundless. Later, she is told that her heart will be pierced by a sword, and she is given a premonition that she will have to share her Son's passion. Here her life echoes the words of Lamentations 1:12, "O all ye that pass by the way, attend, and see if there be any sorrow like to my sorrow," or of the Canticle of Canticles, "Depart from me, I will weep bitterly: labour not to comfort me." Always again, she is prayerful, silent, recollected, loving, seemingly in the background and yet gloriously in the foreground, through her maternity.

She alone combines two unique privileges given to women: virginity and maternity. By her virginity, she testifies to her total donation to her God and creator. She knows that the mysterious garden of her womb is to be kept untouched by man, so that not only is the veil of her virginity untorn before she conceives Christ but is kept so after His birth; for no one was worthy to inhabit in the holy place where He had found a human refuge during nine months. Women have to choose between biological motherhood and virginity. Both callings are magnificent, but they are not compatible. Just as the priesthood and maternity cannot be united in one and the same person, so God has decided that biological motherhood and virginity cannot be united. He makes one unique exception: for the sweet flower of Nazareth that He has chosen to be the mother of His Son. "Thou are blessed and venerable, O Virgin Mary, who without any violation of purity, wert found the mother of our Saviour. O virgin mother of God He whom the whole world is unable to contain being made man, enclosed Himself in thy womb."[166]

But Mary's virginity and motherhood also manifest the immense spiritual fecundity of virginity. The virgin who consecrates herself to God in total donation is not and cannot remain barren. She, too, is called to be called mother, but her motherhood is of a spiritual nature, and for this reason is open to the world. A biological mother can, in exceptional cases, bring twenty-four children into the world (Saint Catherine of Sienna was the twenty-fourth child of Lapa). A consecrated virgin is called upon to be the mother of millions of souls whose sorrows she carries in her heart and to whom she hopes to help give birth in eternal life. Paul Evdokimov writes: *"La femme tient avant tout ce charisme maternel d'enfanter le Christ dans les âmes des hommes"* ("The special maternal charism is to give birth to Christ in men's souls").[167]

Mary is the one creature who unconditionally accepted her creatureliness with all its limitations and weaknesses, with the trust that the Lord, who has seen the humility of His servant, would accomplish great things in her soul. Those women who have repeatedly been deemed "weak" find in Mary their special title of glory. How sweet to be weak when one is carried by the all-loving and all-powerful God who can do all things. That this "weakness," this gentleness and frailty (she is called in the liturgy "the meekest of the meek") is transfigured by grace is powerfully expressed in the liturgy in which the sweet flower of Nazareth is referred to as "an army set in array."[168] Mary must be "terrible as an army with banners."[169]

"God has never made or formed but one enmity; but it is an irreconcilable one: it is between Mary, His worthy mother, and the devil; between the children and servants of the blessed virgin and the children and instruments of Lucifer. Satan fears Mary not only more than all angels and men, but in some sense more than God Himself. It is not that the anger, the hatred, and the power of God are not infinitely greater than those of the Blessed Virgin, for the perfections of Mary are limited; but it is because Satan, being proud, suffers infinitely more from being beaten and punished by a little and humble handmaid of God, and her humility humbles him more than the divine power. The devils fear one of her sighs for a soul more than the prayers of all the saints, and one of her menaces against them more than all other torments."[170]

No other human being has been given such a power, because no other human being was more anxious to love and to serve. The liturgy has this admirable prayer: *"Adonai, Domine, Deus magne et mirabilis, qui dedisti salutem in manu feminae, exaudi preces servorum tuorum"* ("O Adonai, Lord God, great and wonderful, Who didst give salvation by the hand of a woman; hear the prayers of Thy servants"), the Saturday before the Fourth Sunday of September. This willingness to give everything and to feel privileged in doing so explains why Mary is the "one who refutes all heresies." Fathers of the Church, Doctors of the Church, truly Catholic theologians, are all called upon to defend Catholic orthodoxy. But it is the humble Virgin of Nazareth who refutes *all the errors* that the enemy of man keeps spreading, and sometimes, alas, through the very theologians, priests, and others who have the special mission of defending revealed truth. "But what a mystery that poor, weak humanity, inferior to the angels by nature, should be chosen to give to the angels their king and their queen."[171] Every woman should tremble with gratitude when reading these words which highlight so powerfully the dignity that, through Mary, they have been given in the economy of redemption.

The perfume of Mary's purity has attracted innumerable souls, anxious to offer to God the "rich worth of your virginity."[172] She has revealed to the "weak sex" the greatness and sublimity of femininity. In the light of what has been said, one must marvel at the fact that the feminists have succeeded in convincing so many women that the Roman Catholic Church is sexist and looks down upon them. In fact, the contrary is true. She has exalted the status of women in a unique fashion, and the fact that they have no "power" in the Church is once again a sign of God's special love for the "weak" sex. It is safer to obey than to command, and the one truly worthy to be a leader is not only the one who has learned to obey, but the one who much prefers to do so, and only reluctantly—under the cross—accepts to give orders. This is a truth that has been constantly repeated by the Church. Romano Guardini writes: "Christianity has always placed the life struggling for inner truth and ultimate love above that intent on exterior action, even the most courageous and excellent. It has always valued silence more highly than words, purity of intent more than success, the magnanimity of love more than the effect of labor."[173] The greatest victory was achieved at Calvary at the very moment of what seemed to be the ultimate defeat, with the death of the One who was obedient unto death.

A small story: Many years ago, a young Jewish man, a student of my husband, found his way to the Church. He became a Carthusian monk and after having received his formation at the Grande Chartreuse and having spent some time in England, he was sent to the United States to the first Carthusian monastery in this country. He became prior and was reelected and reelected every single time the monks voted, for some twenty-five years. One day, I received a letter from him, informing me that—after having attended a meeting at the Grande Chartreuse—it was decided unanimously that when a superior had reached a certain age and had exercised the charge of superior for many years, he should not be reelected. He ended this brief note by saying: "Finally, I can once again be a real Carthusian and obey." This is the victory of the supernatural.

It is appropriate to end this short work dedicated to the beauty of femininity by remarking that pagan art in various countries has honored the male genitals and developed a phallic cult still visible today in monuments and sculptures. The moment the Church gained ascendency, she waged a relentless war against this aberration. But She has introduced a prayer, repeated millions of times every single day for centuries, in which the female organ *par excellence* — the womb — is exalted: "Blessed is the fruit of thy Womb, Jesus."

Indeed, it is a privilege to be a woman.

References

1 See: *Edith Stein,* Paris: Editions du Seuil, pp. 95, 101.
2 Population Research Institute, Front Royal, VA. Tel. 540-622-5240.
3 Sirach 7:27; Isaiah 13:18; Ezra 30:16.
4 Simone de Beauvoir, *The Second Sex* (New York: Alfred Knopf, 1993), p. 140.
5 *Ibid.,* p. 51.
6 *Ibid.,* p. 456.
7 *Ibid.,* p. 518.
8 G. K. Chesterton, *What is Wrong with the World* (New York: Sheed and Ward, 1956), p. 197.
9 de Beauvoir, *op. cit.,* p. 105.
10 G. K. Chesterton, quoted in "Woman and the Philosophers," Chesterton Review, XI.1, February 1985, Saskatchewan, Canada, p. 20.
11 Sigmund Freud, quoted in de Beauvoir, *op. cit.,* p. 46.
12 Aristotle, *The Generation of Animals,* IV-2. 766 b–33.
13 Sirach 25:14.
14 Sirach 25:15.
15 Sirach 25:23.
16 Sirach 26:7.
17 Sirach 42:14.
18 Ecclesiastes 7:28.

19 Sirach 42:14.

20 Yerushalmi, Sotah 3–4.

21 Quoted in Buytendÿk, *ibid., La Femme* (Paris: Desclée de Brouwer, 1954), p. 66.

22 Martin Luther, *Works.* 12.94 and 20.84 (Germany: Weimer Press, 1883).

23 William Shakespeare, *Hamlet: Prince of Denmark;* Act I, Scene 2.

24 Quoted in Buytendÿk, *op. cit.,* p. 74.

25 *Ibid.,* p. 70.

26 Friedrich Nietzsche, *Thus Spake Zarathustra* (Stuttgart: Alfred Kroener Verlag, 1988), Band 75–91, p. 71.

27 *Selections from Schopenhauer* (New York: Charles Scribner, Modern Student's Library, 1928), p. 435.

28 *Ibid.,* p. 441.

29 Quoted in Norbert Guterman, *A Book of French Quotations* (New York: Doubleday Anchor, 1990), p. 327.

30 André Maurois, *Ariel ou la Vie de Shelley* (Paris: B. Grasset, 1946), p. 213.

31 Quoted in Buytendÿk, *op. cit.,* p. 73.

32 Proverbs 31:10.

33 Sirach 7:19.

34 See: Schiller, *Wuerde der Frauen* (Dignity of Women).

35 In Buytendÿk, *op. cit.,* p. 279.

36 de Beauvoir, *op. cit.,* p. 229.

37 *Ibid.,* pp. 55, 112.

38 *Ibid.,* p. 55.

39 Tatiana Goricheva, *Talking About God is Dangerous* (New York: Cross Road, 1988), p. 86–87.

40 Søren Kierkegaard, *Works of Love* (New York: Harper Torchbooks, 1951), p. 139.

41 Chesterton, *What is Wrong with the World? op. cit.,* p. 148.

42 Quoted in Guterman, *op. cit.*, p. 151.

43 Søren Kierkegaard, *Either-Or*, (written under the pseudonym of Victor Eremita) (Princeton, NJ: Princeton University Press, 1946), p. ii, 77.

44 Friedrich Nietzsche, *Menschliches, allzu Menschliches*, *Ibid.*, I.II, 265.

45 Friedrich Nietzsche, *Ecce Homo*, *ibid.*, Band 77, p. 344.

46 Kierkegaard, *Either-Or*, p. ii, 260–61. It is noteworthy that Free Masonry encouraged and furthered the feminist revolution. See: Pierre Virion, *Mysterium Iniquitatis* (Rennes, France: Editions Saint Michel, 1967), p. 141.

47 de Beauvoir, *op. cit.*, p. 97.

48 *Ibid.*, p. 172.

49 *Ibid.*, p. 171.

50 Luke 2:7.

51 Philippians 2:10.

52 Luke 2:11.

53 Matthew 2:11.

54 Guéranger, *The Liturgical Year*, Volume V (Westminster, MD: The Newman Press, 1949), p. 172.

55 *Glimpses of the Church Fathers*, edited by Claire Russell (London: Scepter, 1996), p. 506.

56 Kierkegaard, *op. cit.*, p. ii, 174.

57 Luke 23:26.

58 Isaiah 53:5.

59 My husband used to remark that many of the most fanatical Nazis were recruited among extremely mediocre individuals who, upon discovering that they were "blond beasts," suddenly put on airs, and claimed superiority over very talented individuals who did not enjoy the "privilege" of belonging to the Nordic race.

60 See: *First Things* (November 1999):In a letter to the editor, Robert Alpert excoriates Pius XII for his "silence" during World War II. According to the author, this great pope should have preferred reprisals against Christians rather than keeping a cowardly silence. He writes: "It is central to Christian belief as I understand it, that the time of trial may come when we must risk and if need be offer our lives" (p. 12). Pius XII had already denounced anti-Semitism in 1938 in *Mit Brennender Sorge.* Continued re-denunciation could have magnified the horror, not only by increasing Hitler's hatred of the chosen people, but also by meaninglessly sacrificing innumerable Christians. The Pope could not command martyrdom, as he said to my husband in a private audience in January 1936. According to Mr. Alpert, Pius XII should have "forced" German Catholics to martyrdom. This heroic death must be freely chosen. A true Christian does not judge the *intentions* of others, does not excoriate them for not being "heroic." He should pray for the grace to be heroic himself when the situation calls for martyrdom. The words of Christ, "Do not judge and you shall not be judged," apply in this case.

61 Søren Kierkegaard, *Concluding Unscientific Postscript* (Princeton, NJ: Princeton University Press, 1992), p. 386.

62 See: Wisdom 2:16 and 2:21. Peter Singer's appointment as professor of bioethics at Princeton University — the apostle of "animals' rights" and basically of the equality of men and animals — eloquently illustrates this tendency toward moral blindness.

63 Wisdom 1:12.

64 See: Dietrich von Hildebrand, *The Trojan Horse in the City of God* (Manchester, NH: Sophia Institute Press, 1999).

65 I Corinthians 1:19.

66 Dietrich von Hildebrand, *op. cit.*, challenges the concept of "modern man," pp. 153–154.

67 Quoted in Paul Evdokimov, *La Femme et le Salut du Monde* (Paris: Casterman, 1958), p. 162.

68 Louis Fisher, *The Life of Mahatma Ghandi* (New York: Harper Collins, 1983), p. 179.

69 *Ibid.*, p. 427.

70 Michael Scammell, *Solzhenitsyn* (New York: W. W. Norton Co., 1984), p. 726.

71 Joan Haslip, *Catherine the Great* (New York: Putnam, 1976), p. 170.

72 Isolde Kurz, *Der Meister von San Francesco*, p. 70.

73 F. W. Foerster, *Erlebte Weltgeschichte* (Nürnberg: Glock und Lutz, 1953), p. 444.

74 Pearl Buck, *My Several Worlds* (New York: John Day, 1957), p. 152.

75 Pearl Buck, *The Dragon Seed* (New York: John Day, 1941), p. 95.

76 *Ibid.*, p. 232.

77 Albert Speer, *Inside the Third Reich* (New York: Mac-Millan, 1970), p. 146.

78 Kierkegaard. *Either-Or,* ii, p. 56.

79 *Ibid.*, p. 260–261.

80 Nietzsche, *Beyond Good and Evil, ibid.*, Band 76, p. 167.

81 Nietzsche, *Die Unschuld des Werdens, ibid.*, Band 82, p. 311.

82 Gabriel Marcel, *Homo Viator: Prolégomènes à une Métaphysique de l'Espérance* (Paris: Aubier, 1947), p. 175.

83 Matthew 20:28.

84 Saint Teresa of Avila, *Vie de Sainte Térèse* (Paris: Julien Lanier, 1852), Chapter XL, p. 607.

85 Ratisbonne, *Saint Bernard of Clairvaux* (Rockford, IL: Tan, 1991), p. 222–223.

86 2 Peter 3:10.

87 de Beauvoir, *op. cit.*, p. 456.

88 1 Peter 3:7.

89 See: D. von Hildebrand's *Man and Woman* (Chicago, IL: Franciscan Herald Press, 1966), p. 63.

90 Paul Evdokimov, *La Femme et le Salut du Monde* (Paris: Casterman, 1958), p. 159.

91 Dom Raymond Thibaut, *Abbot Columba Marmion* (St. Louis, MS: Herder Book Co., 1961), p. 231.

92 *Ibid.*, p. 607.

93 Goethe, *Faust,* Part I, Verse 3585.

94 II Corinthians 12:10.

95 Guéranger, *The Liturgical Year,* Volume 4 (Westminster, MD: The Newman Press, 1949), p. 246.

96 Why are we so moved at the sight of babies? A "normal" human being is deeply touched by the weakness of a newborn whose survival depends upon the constant care of others. Their weakness is a call to handle them with infinite gentleness and tenderness. It is one of the most disastrous consequences of abortion that many are those in our society today who have extinguished in their sick hearts this tender love for the most helpless of creatures: the baby in the womb. The harm that the practice of abortion has done to the human heart is inestimable. We could define abortionists and those blind to the horror of abortion as "those who have no heart," no tenderness toward the weak.

97 Saint Augustine, *Confessions,* Book VIII, 12.

98 Psalm 118:71.

99 Virgil, *Aeneid,* I, 462.

100 *Tridentine Missal,* September 15.
101 See: Dietrich von Hildebrand, *The Heart* (Chicago, IL: Franciscan Herald Press, 1965), Chapter IV.
102 Blaise Pascal, *Pensées texte de Léon Brunschvicg; introduction par Emile Faguet* (Paris: Nelson, 1949), p. 277.
103 *Ibid.,* p. 267.
104 *Ibid.,* p. 272.
105 Chesterton, *ibid.,* p. 163.
106 Søren Kierkegaard, *Concluding Unscientific Postscript* (Princeton, NJ: Princeton University Press, 1941), p. 268.
107 Chesterton, *What is Wrong with the World,* p. 113.
108 Esther 5.
109 Dom Guéranger, *The Liturgical Year,* Volume 4, p. 267.
110 Genesis 6.
111 Ratisbonne, *op. cit.,* p. 105.
112 Quoted *ibid.,* p. 105.
113 Søren Kierkegaard, *Fear and Trembling and Sickness unto Death,* Appendix (Garden City, NJ: Doubleday Anchor, 1954), p. 215.
114 I Corinthians 1:25.
115 II Corinthians 2:30.
116 II Corinthians 7:5
117 Saint Augustine, *Confessions* VI, 8.
118 Saint Augustine, *Contra Letteras Petiliani* iii II. Quoted in Guéranger, Volume V, p. 10.
119 *The Story of a Soul,* French Edition: Carmel de Lisieux, 1957, p. 163.
120 I Peter 5:6.
121 Chesterton, *What is Wrong with the World,* p. 144.
122 *Bartlett's Familiar Quotations* (Boston, MA: Little, Brown and Co., 1947), p. 877.
123 I Corinthians 4:7.

124 Søren Kierkegaard, *Fear and Trembling and Sickness unto Death*, (Garden City, NJ: Doubleday, 1954), p. 205.

125 Gertrud von le Fort, *The Eternal Woman, The Woman in Time [and] Timeless Woman* (Milwaukee: Bruce Publishing Co., 1962), p. 51.

126 On a purely secular plane, it is noteworthy that Descartes chose to write his famous *Discourse on the Method* in French and not in Latin, so that this work would be accessible to women whose minds are less cluttered by theories and preformed ideas, that is, because they are more receptive.

127 D. von Hildebrand, *The Heart* (Chicago, IL: Franciscan Herald Press, 1977), 2, pp. 47, 75.

128 *Ibid.*, p. 50.

129 In this context, we cannot address the interesting question whether pleasures and pains as experienced by persons differ widely from the same feelings experienced by animals, because for man—a person—suffering has meaning, whereas, to use the profound words of Dante, animals do not know the "why": "...e lo 'mperché non sanno." (*Divine Comedy*, "Purgatory," Canto iii, verse 84).

130 D. von Hildebrand, *op. cit.*, p. 52 ff.

131 G. K. Chesterton, *Orthodoxy* (Garden City, NJ: Image Book, 1959), p. 55.

132 See: Saint Augustine, *De Doctrina Christiana*, I–27.

133 Plato, *Laws* II, 653.

134 Dietrich von Hildebrand, *Christian Ethics*, (New York: D. McKay Co., 1953), Chapter 25.

135 *The Journals of Kierkegaard*, translated by Alexander Dru (New York: Harper, 1958), p. 215.

136 Ivan Goncharov, *Oblomov* (New York: Dutton, 1960), p. 204.

137 Ezekiel II:19 and 36:26.

138 Proverbs 23:26.

139 Jeremiah 17:9.

140 Saint Térèse of Avila, *ibid.*, Chapter XXVII.

141 There is no doubt that Dietrich von Hildebrand is one of the great champions of the role and importance of affectivity in human and religious life. It is noteworthy, however, that he is also the person who has analyzed the dangers that illegitimate feelings play in our lives. See: *Transformation in Christ*, pp. 255, 339.

142 *Litany of the Sacred Heart.*

143 Ratisbonne, *op. cit.*, p. 225.

144 Canticle of Canticles 2:5.

145 Saint Bonaventure, *The Mind's Road to God*, Part 1 (New York: The Library of Liberal Arts, 1953), p. 8.

146 Thessalonians 5:17.

147 See also: D. von Hildebrand, *Transformation in Christ*, "Recollection and Contemplation," Chapter VI.

148 Canticle of Canticles 4:12.

149 Saint Augustine, *On Virginity*, X, 10 (Paris: Desclée de Brouwer, 1939), III, p. 213.

150 Shakespeare, A *Midsummer Night's Dream*, Act II, Scene 1.

151 Psalms 113.

152 Matthew 21:31.

153 Chesterton, *op. cit.*, p. 192.

154 *Ibid*, Chapter I, p. 3 PP.

155 Quote *Congressional Record*, Volume 113 (1967), pp. 28848–28849.

156 See: Dietrich von Hildebrand's *Purity* (Steubenville, OH: Franciscan University of Steubenville Press, 1995), Chapter 1, p. 3.

157 Immanuel Kant, *Fundamental Principles of the Metaphysic of Morals* (New York: The Library of Liberal Arts, 1949), p. 46.

158 Plato, *Phaedo*, xxxiii, p. 83.

159 Saint Augustine, *Confessions* I, 12.

160 Evdokimov, *op. cit.*, p. 162.

161 Von le Fort, *op. cit.*, p. 78.

162 Cf. Gereon Goldman, *On the Shadows of His Wings* (San Francisco: Ignatius Press, 1999), pp. 104–105. Also: Eugenio Corti, *The Red Horse* (San Francisco: Ignatius Press, 2000), p. 255.

163 Saint Augustine, *Commentary on the Psalms* (Psalm 31), Volume II (New York: Newman Press, 1961), p. 87.

164 Luke 5:8.

165 Pascal, *Pensées texte de Léon Brunschvicg; introduction par Emile Faguet* (Paris: Nelson, 1949), p. 416.

166 *Litany of the Blessed Virgin.*

167 Evdokimov, *op. cit.*, p. 220.

168 Canticle of Canticles 6:3.

169 Canticle of Canticles 6:4.

170 Guéranger, *op. cit.*, p. 205.

171 *Ibid*, p. 169.

172 Shakespeare, A *Midsummer Night's Dream*, Act II, Scene 1.

173 Romano Guardini, *The Lord* (Chicago, IL: Regency, 1954), p. 194.